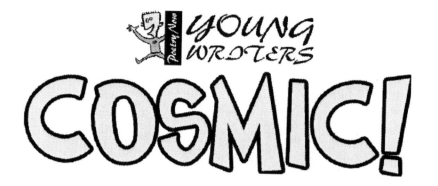

BRISTOL

Edited by Carl Golder

First published in Great Britain in 1998 by
POETRY NOW YOUNG WRITERS
1-2 Wainman Road, Woodston,
Peterborough, PE2 7BU
Telephone (01733) 230748

HB ISBN 0 75430 069 2
SB ISBN 0 75430 070 6

FOREWORD

With over 63,000 entries for this year's Cosmic competition, it has proved to be our most demanding editing year to date.

We were, however, helped immensely by the fantastic standard of entries we received, and, on behalf of the Young Writers team, thank you.

The Cosmic series is a tremendous reflection on the writing abilities of 8-11 year old children, and the teachers who have encouraged them must take a great deal of credit.

We hope that you enjoy reading *Cosmic Bristol* and that you are impressed with the variety of poems and style with which they are written, giving an insight into the minds of young children and what they think about the world today.

CONTENTS

Daniel Dorrington	17
Shaun Marsh	17
Emily Moore	18
Victoria Mullan	18
Jon Roche	18
Ryan Turner	19

Blaise Primary School

Amber Davies	19
David Phillips	20
Rochelle Chapman	20
Emily Hayward	21
Matt Jeakings	21
Brett Davies	22
Thomas Sheppard	22
Nikela Roberts	23
Shalney Baker	23
Jonathan Barnett	24
Christopher Parsons	24
Victoria Smith	25
Charlotte Johnson	25
Sun Jee	26
Jenny Meredith	26
Paul Garland	27
Cassie Rankin	28
Bobby Widdowfield	29
Kieran Bligh	29
Abbey Wyllie	30
Jayne Threadgold	30
Oliver Guiver	31
Jade Stevens	31
Cayleigh Williams	32
Tony Brown	33
Jade Guiver	33
Jenna Parsons	34
Kirsty Davison	34
Mark Searle	35
John Roberts	36

Fairfield School

Edward Bartholomew	88
Sophie Perrin	89
Jennie Grene	89
George Wrightson	90
Tom Henley	90
Tim Power	91
Thomas Wright	91
Caroline Organ	92
Harriet Amelia Smith	92
David Royce	93
Grace Perrin	93

Gracefield Preparatory School

Peter Edwards	94
James Flanagan	94
Luke Bachhuber	95
Jennifer L K Hawke	96
James Blackburn	97
Sophie Arnold	97
Timothy Sadler	98
Ben Mealing	98
Andrew Gunningham	99
Stephen Hooper	100

Hambrook Primary School

Eleanor Smith	101
Harriet Lamb	101
Kerina Evans	102
James Baldwin	102
Sebastian David Pike	103
Stuart Payne	104
Georgina Hooper	104
Grace McLarty	105
Rosie Moscrop	105
Jason Dayment	106
Adam Slade	106
Hollie Godrich	107

Sophie Coleman	107
Lydia Clayphan Turner	108
Emma Lerway	108
Louise Harmer	109
Richard Clay	109
Ben Glastonbury	110
Frank Jayne	110
Eliza George	111
Joshua Beale	111
Michael Crotch-Harvey	112
Charlotte Wall	113

Headley Park Primary School

Lucy Harvey	113
Amy Barnes	114
Charlotte Harris	114
Katie Daly	155
Melissa Cockle	115

Henbury Court Junior School

Bradley Roy Clark	115
Kayleigh Hayward	116
Christopher Parton	116
Zoe Uzzell	117
Tom Alexander	117
John Lyons	118
Ben Willshire	118
Benn Goodmore	119
Jonathan Verdon	119
Jennifer Smith	120
Alexander Wike	120
Lucinda Stokes	121
Jason Love	121
Justin Barry	122
Tom Nightingale	122
Lauren Graves	123
Rachael Cox	123
Amy Evans	124

Henleaze Junior School

Katrina Hornsey	159
Alison Grist	159
Byron Stadden	160
Kirstie Hillman	160
Faye Harvey	160
Jordan Paul	161
Jonathan Morgan	161
Edmund Hinton	161
Kay Titiloye	162
Carmelo Cocchiara	162
Laura Cass	163
Stephanie Aldrich	163
Sasha Squires	164

Holymead Junior School

Matthew Grant	164
Rebecca Budd	165
Rebecca Taylor	165
Michal Eddolls	166
Scott Saunders	166
Josh Short	166
Cate Totney	167
Andrew Webber	167
Nicholas Cockram	168
Rachel Witcombe	168
Steven Adams	168
Jenny Edgecombe	169
Katie Williams	169
Laura Hudd	170
Stacey Roberts	170
Lisa Collier	171
Jennifer Skuse	171
Lucy Egan	171
Emily Thompson	172
Richard Harley	172
David Swatton	173
Alexandra Farley	173
Samantha Orchard	174

Stephen Gowing	193
Amy Bush	193
Jonathan Tucker	194
Lauren Cockburn	194
Emily Graupner	195
Emma Newport	196
Amy Tilley	196
Jerome Scholefield	197
Zoe Davis	198
Gareth Alvis	198
Stacey Searle	199
Ruth Evans	199
Jessica Wells	200
Tom Edwards	200
Gemma Louise Davenport	201
Amanda Dunleavy	202
Jodie Chilcott	202

Rodford Junior School

David Smith	203
Tim Skuse	203
Jason Andrew Summers	204
Janie Porter	204
Scott Smith	204
Scott Walker	205
Lydia Amesbury	205
Jake Steeds	206
James Darren Templeton	206
Clare Barnes	207
Amy Messenger	207
Scott Perkins	208
Bethany Portingale	209
Heidi Dracup	209
Russell Reynolds	210
Ashley Matthews	210
Beth Ainslie	211
Stephanie Biggin	211
Jason Timbrell	212

Sefton Park Junior School

Cecily Evans-Blondel	250
Jade Templer	250
Daryl Allen	250
Marlon Lorenzo Gayle	251
Annabel Wilson	251
Mercedes Villalba	252
Alice Eddie	252

Summerhill Junior School

Gemma Gray	253
Laura Summerhayes	253
Ayisha Grant	254
Ashley Porter	254
Alec Cridland	255
Carl Winstanley	255
Charlotte Evans	255
Kyli Morgan	256
Anna Francis	256
Jenna Webley	257
Tina Coombes	257
James Harty	257
Anna Phillips	258
Richard Bower	258
Cirsty Inker	258
Georgina Cox	259
Rocky Hopkins	259
Rebecca Knight	260
Eugenie Brain	260
Matthew Owen	261
Teri Gauge	262
David Lock	262
Natalie Hart	263
Rebecca Flanagan	263
Sam Bracey	264
Jake Edwards	264
Curtis Pinkett	265
Christopher Takle	265

THE POEMS

IN FRANCE

I was waiting to get in the car
I went in the car
And the car went off
It was a long way to Dover
But I was there
I went around the shops
And it was Tuesday
I waited to go on the 'sea cat'
I went to France
I went to the shops
Went to a castle
Went swimming
Went eating
Went back home.

Sam Brown (7)
Abbotswood Junior School

MAN UNITED

When I went to Manchester
I went in the shops
I bought a Man United kit
I went in the stadium
I felt cold and excited
And amazed and shivery
Then I saw Ryan Giggs
And Andy Cole.

Jodie Buckle (7)
Abbotswood Junior School

THE ALIEN

I got in a spaceship
and went to the moon.
I saw an alien
it went in its spaceship.
I said it must be afraid
I never knew aliens
were afraid of people.
I got in my spaceship
and went to Mars.
'Are there any Mars bars?'
I said to David.
It was time to go home.
So I got in a spaceship and went
to the earth.

Rebecca Jevons (7)
Abbotswood Junior School

TIME TO GO TO WESTON

One day,
I went to Weston,
the seaside,
on the train.
When we got there,
I went on
the ghost train
and the roller-coaster.
I ate an iced lolly
and some candyfloss.

Natalie Britton (7)
Abbotswood Junior School

DISNEYLAND

One day
I went
To Disneyland,
America.
I saw Mickey.
He was very funny.
Then I saw
One of the rides.
I really wanted
To go on one.
I wished
I could go on it.
It was a very big roller-coaster,
That was fast,
But very daft.
It spun
Round and round,
In the town,
It went up and down,
It almost touched the ground.
When I went home
I felt so wizzy
That I was dizzy.

Carly Jordan (8)
Abbotswood Junior School

HOLIDAYS

When I went to a amphitheatre
in Wales last week,
I saw the fighting ground.
It was great.
I said 'Can I come again?'
'No' my nan said.
'I wish I could.'
'No' my grandad said.
'Please, I begged.'
'Oh no!' they both said.
My grandad told me all about it.
How the slaves had to fight animals
and other animals had to fight.
It was getting late.
So we had to go home.

Lauren Ayres (8)
Abbotswood Junior School

FAIRY

Jake and Terry came around;
We went to the pictures to see a film
It was all about fairies.
We had popcorn and Coke.
I enjoyed the film very much.
When I went to bed and fell asleep
I dreamt I made a house for the fairy.

Charlotte Privett-Saunders (8)
Abbotswood Junior School

THE MATCH

In the holidays I wished I was going to Manchester
to see Manchester United V Blackburn Rovers
and the score was 3-2 to Manchester United.
At the end of the match I felt very proud of
Manchester.
When I went home I fell asleep, I dreamt of
the next match I would go and see.

Lee Sidney (8)
Abbotswood Junior School

AT DISNEYLAND PARIS

I went to Disneyland, Paris,
Tigger jumped all over my mum
And I went on a pirate ship
I had a photo with Mickey Mouse
but the photo did not come out
because there was no film in.
So I did not have that photo,
at Disneyland, Paris.

Luke Haddow (7)
Abbotswood Junior School

I WENT TO WESTON

I went to Weston in the holidays
I went to Brean sands.
Me and my mum and dad
saw a shipwreck.
Then I had some chips.
I had fun.

Simon Cottrell (7)
Abbotswood Junior School

THE SPACESHIP

One day I found a spaceship.
I went in the spaceship
It was amazing.
There was a robot,
In the spaceship
An alien.
I pressed a button
It made the spaceship
Go to the moon.
It was made of cheese
And it tasted excellent.

Daniel Rushent (7)
Abbotswood Junior School

DISNEYLAND

I went to Disneyland.
And saw a Disney fan
She had pink and purple stripes bright
She saw her nan she's a fan of Disneyland!
She felt very happy being a Disney fan.
Her nan felt excited
And got a sun tan
And began to fan herself.
And at the end of the holiday
We went home in a van.

Laura Mulcahy (8)
Abbotswood Junior School

THE ROMAN LIGHTHOUSE

I wish I could see
A Roman lighthouse
And I would go inside
I'd touch some things
But not the fragile things
Because they might break
So I went up the stairs
I saw a man and his wife
I said 'Hello,' they said 'Come with us
to the magic room.'
'Magic room' I said
'I've never been to a magic room'
'Well this is very special to us'
said the lady
'Ok then
I promise
I won't touch anything
Excuse me
have you got anything'
'Yes we have got bread and butter pudding'
'Yum, yum'
I said.
'I like bread and butter pudding'
I ate it all up
Then I left the lighthouse
and went home again.

Amber Rickards (8)
Abbotswood Junior School

THE MATCH

I went to a Liverpool match
And I saw Michael Owen
And Fowler kicked the ball
On my head.
I ran on the pitch when the
Match finished.
I screamed 'Go Liverpool, go, go Liverpool,
go Michael Owen, go, go Fowler!'
I shouted, 'Michael Owen you're the best.'
I got Michael Owen's autograph and
I went home
I felt good because I saw Liverpool
And best of all Michael Owen.

Faye Roberts (8)
Abbotswood Junior School

WHAT'S ON HOLIDAY

When I went on holiday
The sand was golden
And I saw a crab
The volcanoes were erupting at
All times since the Romans
Palm trees, big, tall
With large leaves
And hard to bend
Little lizards looking for food.

Dean Lewis (7)
Abbotswood Junior School

THE MATCH!

Yesterday I went
to a football match.
Man United won.
I felt delighted!

I wish they had scored
1,000,000 goals!

Daniel Wells (7)
Abbotswood Junior School

MY NEW ROOM

My new room
is yellow and blue.
It didn't take my daddy
very long to do.
The yellow reminds me of the *hot, hot* sun,
because I like to run, run, run.
Blue is the colour
of our school uniform,
Which looks good
and helps us to perform.

Verity Collier (9)
Begbrook Primary School

COSMIC

The aliens are,
driving in a space car,
they have travelled very far,
from their planet that looks like a star.
They're going to invade,
on a crusade.
They've landed on earth,
by some turf.
They got out of their car,
and went into a bar.
They're going to invade,
on a crusade.
The police were outside the bar,
when they saw the space car,
and they thought they were dreaming,
while they watched the light beaming.
They saw some spaceships,
and they looked like pips.
They're going to invade,
on a crusade.
They went into shops,
and killed all of the cops.
People were dying,
while aliens were flying.
The aliens are invading,
while the world is fading.
They're going to invade,
on a crusade.
The aliens are going back,
with a little haystack.

Sunil Singh (10)
Begbrook Primary School

PLUTO IS BURNING BRIGHT RED

P luto is burning bright red.
L ooking up at the sky you can see the stars.
A steroids orbit the sun.
N eptune is virtually made up of hydrogen.
E arth is our planet we live on, surrounded by space.
T elescopes, if you look through them, you can see Saturn.
S aturn has three rings which are flat.

Cassie Green (8)
Begbrook Primary School

STORM, STORM, STORM, STORM

Grease the bowl,
Toss in 6 tablespoons of strong wind,
Knead the clouds,
Add black wax,
Throw in an ounce of lightning,
Sprinkle on half a dozen sounds of thunder,
Puff up the clouds when the wax has hardened,
Add 1½ tablespoons of rain,
Heat up for about 2 minutes,
Add the rest of the black wax for extra blackness,
Mix it all together thoroughly,
Shake it, not stir,
Thoroughly cook it on gas mark 120°C.

Now ready for a downpour!

Michael Hares (10)
Bishopsworth Junior School

STORM

Start with a wide place,
Throw in some mountains,
Sprinkle on some snow,
Grate in some lightning.
Add a quarter of a teaspoon of rain,
Shake in some clouds,
Add dark black dye,
Whisk in some fog.
Add 1½ tablespoons of thunder,
Mix in some mud.
Blend them together,
Turn down the heat.
After that throw in 7oz of people,
And fold in some umbrellas.

Anne Lawrence (9)
Bishopsworth Junior School

RECIPE FOR A STORM

Throw in some blowing wind,
Throw in some black clouds,
Sprinkle in some rain,
Mix in some thunder,
Mix in some lightning,
Bend it till smooth,
You will have a storm.

Abigail Hooper (10)
Bishopsworth Junior School

RECIPE FOR A STORM

A storm comes over a school
the clouds getting darker and darker.
Thunder goes *boom!* Blending in
with the rain.
Fog falls down and down so no one
can peek through.
Hailstones fall and fall.
Suddenly stop for a nap.
The hailstones stop and snow pours
down and down for the end of the
storm.
The sun comes out and heats the
world right up.

Shaun Attwood (10)
Bishopsworth Junior School

STORM!

Add black food colouring to the 3 clouds,
Add a teaspoon of rain and
throw on *one* thunder,
Crack on the lightning
Add a sparkle from the lightning,
And now add a couple of electrocuted people.
Now mix and put it in the boiling sea
For five minutes.
Then you should have a crashing storm!

James Ellis (10)
Bishopsworth Junior School

RECIPE FOR A STORM

I get out my big black bowl.
Add in the angry thunder storm.
A smidgen of rain.
Combine in some dark old rotten sun.
Add in the wispy dark clouds.
Add the crashing rain.
Tip half a teaspoon of roaring clouds spread
Thinly, add a touch of rain.

Now my recipe
Is
Done!

Kimberley Carr (10)
Bishopsworth Junior School

A RECIPE FOR A STORM

Take a normal size bowl.
Blend in some black clouds.
Sprinkle some rain.
Throw in some heavy wind.
Crack in some thunder and lightning.
Add some more rain.
Stir it up and there is your storm.
Everyone is terrified of this storm.

Andrew Winstanley (11)
Bishopsworth Junior School

RECIPE FOR A STORM

First add some white cloud.
Get some black paint and paint
The clouds black.
Blow in some wind.
Blend, whisk and twist in a tornado.
Blow the wind to over 299 mph.
Swap the sun and snow for a splash of rain.
Now it's time to throw in some lightning
And crack the thunder.
Add 2 ounces of hailstones.
And last of all vanish it all with the complete
Vanish spray.

Andrew Caswell (9)
Bishopsworth Junior School

RECIPE FOR A STORM

Take a teaspoon of rain trickling
down heavier and heavier.
Roll in some thunder.
Whisk in some fog.
A cloud falling down, falling, falling down.
Start the lightning, let it down.
Add some wind getting harder and harder.
The sun comes out, the storm blows away.

Mark Still (9)
Bishopsworth Junior School

RECIPE FOR A STORM

Take some sky,
Add some dark, dark clouds,
Pour in some water,
Sprinkle in some strong wind,
Give it a good mix.
Throw in a few flashes of lightning,
Add two tablespoons of thunder,
Mix with all your might.
Bake for 10 minutes to make it strong.
Serve on a warm plate.

Lisa Grimmer (10)
Bishopsworth Junior School

RECIPE FOR A STORM

Start with a reasonable sized mountain.
Add 3 white clouds.
Throw in crushed black powder,
For the clouds will then turn black.
Roll in some angry lightning.
Sprinkle in some heavy rain.
Clash in the thunder.
Shake in the coldness.
Now you have a freshly made storm.
Serve up to all your friends.

Jenny Farrant (10)
Bishopsworth Junior School

RECIPE FOR A STORM

Throw in some black paint to the clouds.
Throw in a flash of lightning.
Mix in a drop of rain.
Throw yellow paint into the lightning.
A roar of thunder through the clouds.
Add half a teaspoon into the thunder.

Ashley Milkins (9)
Bishopsworth Junior School

RECIPE FOR A STORM

Start off with a spoonful of rain.
Roll some thunder into the rain.
Blend in some misty clouds too.
Sprinkle in some white lightning.

Daniel Dorrington (10)
Bishopsworth Junior School

RECIPE FOR A STORM

Start with six oz of thunder,
Whisk the fog,
Sprinkle on some rain,
Give it a breeze of wind.
Bake the sun on 25 degrees Celsius,
Mix one and a half tablespoons of rain,
Shake the tornado,
Add some grey ink to the clouds.

Shaun Marsh (10)
Bishopsworth Junior School

Recipe For A Storm

Start off with a black sky.
Add half a tablespoon of rain.
Sprinkle in some silver stars.
Blend a bang into it.
Shake some trees into it.
Mix roughly until air comes rushing out. Run, run.
Mix until it gets heavier and heavier.
Drop some snowflakes in and you have a storm.

Emily Moore (10)
Bishopsworth Junior School

Recipe For A Storm

First take a cloud and dip it in dye.
Add to a sky, blue as the sea.
Throw in some thunder as loud as a rocket.
Clash in some lightning as bright as the sun.
Whisk wind ever so aggressive.
Shake in some rain.
Now serve to the earth.

Victoria Mullan (9)
Bishopsworth Junior School

Storm

Pour on 2 tablespoons of rain.
Pour blackcurrant over cotton wool for a cloud.
Throw on the lightning and mix with thunder.
Beat in 5oz of scared people.
Mix with a hurricane
And you have a storm.

Jon Roche (10)
Bishopsworth Junior School

RECIPE FOR A STORM

Begin with a large sized bowl
White clouds turn to black
Throw in some deep rain
And sprinkle with some heavy wind
Add a clash of thunder and lightning
Make a sound of a *boom*
Stir it up and there's your storm
A storm that everyone loves.

Ryan Turner (9)
Bishopsworth Junior School

COLOUR

What is blue?
Blue is the colour of the waves in the sea.
What is pink?
Pink is the colour of a nice strawberry ice-cream
                            which you could eat every day.
What is green?
Green is the colour of beautiful and lovely grass the sun shines on.
What is yellow?
Yellow is the colour of the hot sun shining brightly.
What is indigo?
Indigo is the colour of the night.
What is orange?
Orange is the colour of a nice orange.
What is brown?
Brown is the colour of a lovely tree.
What is amber?
Amber is the colour of a dark stone.

Amber Davies (8)
Blaise Primary School

COLOUR

What is red?
Red is the colour of jelly,
Wobbling on the plate.

What is yellow?
Yellow is the colour of a fish,
Swimming in his fish tank.

What is grey?
Grey is the colour of a wolf,
Howling through the night.

What is white?
White is the colour of porridge,
Which is hot but it is yummy.

What is black?
Black is the colour of a hamster,
Called Runny.

David Phillips (8)
Blaise Primary School

IN THE WOODS

The birds are singing,
The owl is hooting.
The ducks are quacking,
The bird is flying
Over the tree.
The rain is dripping.
The leaves are on the trees.

Rochelle Chapman (8)
Blaise Primary School

COLOUR

What is silver?
Silver is the colour of snowflakes floating in the air.
What is gold?
Gold is the colour of treasure shining bright.
What is black?
Black is the colour of the sky at night.
What is pink?
Pink is the colour of a flamingo.
What is ginger?
Ginger is the colour of a cat's fur.
What is green?
Green is the colour of beautiful grass.
What is yellow?
Yellow is the colour of custard pouring out of the jug.

Emily Hayward (8)
Blaise Primary School

COLOURS

What is red?
Red is the colour of a shiny new car.
What is blue?
Blue is the colour of the summer sky.
What is yellow?
Yellow is the colour of the lovely sun.
What is pink?
Pink is the colour of our beautiful skin.
What is green?
Green is the colour of the grass.

Matt Jeakings (7)
Blaise Primary School

STRANGER WITH THE DRUGS

Drugs are bad
They make you go mad
Stay away from that thug
Yes that one with the drug.
'Hey you! Little boy come here.'
Oh no he's calling my name.
He's trying to play a horrible mind game
I'm walking away as fast as I can.
I'm getting away from that dirty man
He's running towards me
I use my defence
I kick, I scream, I jump over my fence
Heroin, Crack, he's got the lot.
He kept them in this very big pot
He's pushing a drug at me
He said 'It tastes like tea.'
'No! No!' I cried, 'Stay away.'
Just then the police came to save the day
Now that man's in prison.

Brett Davies (11)
Blaise Primary School

COLOURS

Red is the colour of a car.
Orange and black are the colours of a tiger.
Black and white are the colours of a zebra.
Green is the colour of an apple.
Blue is the colour of the sky.

Thomas Sheppard (7)
Blaise Primary School

COLOURS

What is red?
Red is the colour of cars.

What is blue?
Blue is the colour of the sea shining in the sun.

What is orange?
Orange is the colour of oranges, they are bright.

What is yellow?
Yellow is the colour of bananas sitting in the dish.

What is green?
Green is the colour of grass in the field.

What is brown?
Brown is the colour of dogs' tails.

Nikela Roberts (7)
Blaise Primary School

COLOURS

What is yellow?
Yellow is the colour of the sun.
What is red?
Red is the colour of a shiny car.
What is blue?
Blue is the colour of the summer sky.
What is green?
Green is the beautiful grass.
What is pink?
Pink is our beautiful skin.

Shalney Baker (7)
Blaise Primary School

COLOUR

What is red?
Red is the colour of a nice juicy apple.

What is blue?
Blue is the colour of the sea splashing in the wind.

What is yellow?
Yellow is the colour of the nice bright sun.

What is green?
Green is the colour of the grass.

What is orange?
Orange is the colour of a fierce tiger.

What is purple?
Purple is the colour of a juicy plum.

What is gold?
Gold is the colour of a box with shiny treasure inside.

Jonathan Barnett (8)
Blaise Primary School

COLOUR

Red is the colour of a jelly.
Orange is the colour of an orange.
Yellow is the colour of the sun.
Green is the colour of a crayon.
Blue is the colour of a car.
Indigo is the colour of a dark car.
Violet is the colour of a purple bottle.

Christopher Parsons (7)
Blaise Primary School

COLOUR

What is orange?
Orange is the colour of a smooth orange.

What is gold?
Gold is the colour of money.

What is black?
Black is the colour of an X-ray.

What is pink?
Pink is the colour of a rose sitting in the sun.

What is blue?
Blue is the colour of the sea in the summer.

Victoria Smith (7)
Blaise Primary School

COLOUR

What is gold?
Gold is the colour of goldfish swimming.

What is red?
Red is the colour of a strawberry that is nice and sweet.

What is yellow?
Yellow is the colour of the sun shining.

What is green?
Green is the colour of grapes that you eat.

What is purple?
Purple is the colour of a blackberry pie.

Charlotte Johnson (8)
Blaise Primary School

COLOUR

What is red?
Red is the colour of an apple.

What is orange?
Orange is the colour of oranges. I like oranges.

What is yellow?
Yellow is the colour of the shining sun.

What is green?
Green is the colour of my draft book.

What is indigo?
Indigo is the colour of the sea.

What is purple?
Purple is the colour of grapes.

These are six bright colours that I like.

Sun Jee (8)
Blaise Primary School

ALCOHOL

A lcohol can damage your liver,
L eave it alone it can be a killer.
C ider, lager, may taste nice but sooner or later you'll pay the price.
O range juice is
H ealthier and it won't give your words a drunken slur. You're on your
O wn if you want to drink. It takes over your mind so you can't think.
L eave it alone to stay alive, that means this:
Don't drink and drive.

Jenny Meredith (11)
Blaise Primary School

COLOUR

What is red?
Red is the colour of a nice juicy apple.

What is blue?
Blue is the colour of the sea flapping on the sand.

What is green?
Green is the colour of the grass blowing in the breeze.

What is yellow?
Yellow is the colour of the sun shining in the sky.

What is orange?
Orange is the colour of a nice juicy orange.

What is black?
Black is the colour of a dark black sky at night-time.

What is gold?
Gold is the colour of a box of money.

What is silver?
Silver is the colour of snowflakes floating in the air.

What is white?
White is the colour of clouds on a summer's day.

What is brown?
Brown is the colour of a tree swaying in the breeze.

Paul Garland (7)
Blaise Primary School

COLOURS

What is red?
Red is the colour of ripe red cherries.

What is blue?
Blue is the colour of the beautiful summer sky.

What is gold?
Gold is the colour of lovely autumn leaves that have fallen off trees.

What is black?
Black is the colour of a pitch black winter sky at night.

What is green?
Green is the colour of lush green grass in the summer breeze.

What is yellow?
Yellow is the colour of the rising summer sun.

What is grey?
Grey is the colour of elephants swinging their trunks.

What is brown?
Brown is the colour of coconuts that have just fallen off trees.

What is white?
White is the colour of beautiful pure white snow.

What is orange?
Orange is the colour of a carrot that's nice and crunchy.

What is pink?
Pink is the colour of the Pink Panther on television.

Cassie Rankin (7)
Blaise Primary School

BULLIED

I stand in the playground all alone, hoping someone
will play with me.

When people pick teams I point to myself,
hoping someone will pick me but they never do.

They look at me in a mean way and then
they walk away and whisper to their friends.
I look at them and wish that I had a friend too.

I stand in the hall alone and hope someone
will sit by me, but they move away and whisper.

At home time my mum picks me up from
school and says 'How was school?'
'OK.' I tell her.

When I get home I go to my room and I cry
and cry and sometimes I cry myself to sleep.

Bobby Widdowfield (11)
Blaise Primary School

OLD PEOPLE ON THE MOTORWAY IN ENGLAND

We are driving in our car,
I'm Grandpa and she's Grandma.
We are slow and we are pains,
People think we have no brains.
Driving down the motorway,
People yell out 'Go away.'
So all those Grandpas and Grandmas,
Don't listen to those silly youths.
Just drive your careful way.

Kieran Bligh (11)
Blaise Primary School

COLOUR

What is orange?
Orange is the colour of a nice orange.
What is red?
Red is the colour of a rose growing up high.
What is green?
Green is the colour of seaweed.
What is blue?
Blue is the colour of the wonderful summer sky.
What is silver?
Silver is the colour of bits of glitter falling on Christmas cards.
What is yellow?
Yellow is the colour of a ripe banana.
What is purple?
Purple is the colour of a blackberry pie.
What is ginger?
Ginger is the colour of yummy biscuits.
What is white?
White is the colour of snowflakes floating in the sky.
What is grey?
Grey is the colour of a sky on a stormy day.

Abbey Wyllie (8)
Blaise Primary School

BEST FRIENDS

My friend is good, she helps me all the time.
I think she's good and I know she's mine.
She is so good I play with her all the time.
But most of all she's best of all!
Which is Kathryn Winson!

Jayne Threadgold (8)
Blaise Primary School

COLOUR

What is red?
Red is the colour of a nice juicy apple.

What is orange?
Orange is the colour of a beautiful goldfish swimming about.

What is yellow?
Yellow is the colour of a bumble bee, buzz . . .zz . . . zz . . . ing around.

What is blue?
Blue is the colour of fresh drinking water.

What is indigo?
Indigo is the colour of the sky at night.

What is silver?
Silver is the colour of a 10p and 5p piece.

What is gold?
Gold is the colour of the sun setting.

Oliver Guiver (8)
Blaise Primary School

FRIENDSHIP

Show a smile every day
Make sure it never goes away.
If you need someone for a mate
Remember me, it's not too late.
Now you've found me as your friend
I'll stay with you until the end.
Friends are there when you need them most
They're never ever known to boast.

Jade Stevens (10)
Blaise Primary School

IT'S SUMMER TIME

I love summer, it's full of fun,
T he nice long walks on Weston beach.
S chool is out! No time to teach.

S ummertime, let's all play,
U all can have a happy day.
M emories of winter are gone.
M ore and more fun,
E verybody is out in the sun.
R emember summertime.

T eachers out on the beach,
I love summertime,
M um cooks great on the barbecue
E ven me too.

L et's all enjoy summer,
E verybody will find it funner.
T he sun is staying up to play,
S ometimes staying out the way.

E veryone is going down to the beach,
N ever be sad
J oy is being not bad (ill),
O nly stay out till midday,
Y ou will be happier if you obey.

I enjoyed it in the pool, now it's
T ime to go to school,
Why?

Cayleigh Williams (10)
Blaise Primary School

DRUG ABUSE

Stop taking drugs or stop your life
And cut your fag with a knife.
Stop your greed, don't take speed.
If you take E you will dance and prance.
If you take Cocaine you take your chance
If you drink some booze,
Don't choose strong booze.
Drugs are bad like those thugs
Thugs sell drugs. Drugs kill things or anyone else
Who takes them?
Drugs spread like diseases and diseases spread
Like drugs and drugs and diseases kill people
All over the world.

Tony Brown (11)
Blaise Primary School

THE MOONLIT NIGHT

Gleaming silently through the night
Making everything go bright.
It shines like silver and sparkles
Like the sun making light for everyone.
It turns around the dark sky bright
Moonlight shines upon the night.
The world is silently passing by
Gleaming high up in the sky
Bringing the night then to an end
As it silently drifts away
And is ready for another day.

Jade Guiver (10)
Blaise Primary School

DRUG ABUSE CAUSES DEATH

D rugs are danger, stay away.
R un away from smokers and drugs
U didn't care.
G anja is bad.

A bout to die.
B ecause you did the wrong thing.
U didn't do as you should
S tay away from solvents and other things
E arly deaths are tragic.

C igarettes are bad for your lungs
A bout to light a fag.
U think it's cool, as if.
S moking can give you a shorter life.
E verybody can die if they take drugs
S horter lives do come quick.

D eath can come around the corner quickly
E verybody try to stay safe.
A lways keep away from drug dealers
T ake care
H ealthy lives are best.

Jenna Parsons (10)
Blaise Primary School

FRIENDSHIP POEM

Friends bring joy, happiness and trust
Friends are always there for us
Friends bring lots of magic too
Friends will always stay with you.

Friends are really special to me
Friends bring laughter and such glee
Friends aren't like a ragged shoe
Friends are like a pretty view.

Kirsty Davison (10)
Blaise Primary School

CHRISTMAS DAY

Christmas day is always fun
I always wait for my presents to come
Come on presents where have you gone?
I'm waiting for Father Christmas, where has he gone?

He might be here, he might not,
Was I good, or was I not?

I go down stairs to see if Father Christmas is there.
I go back to bed because I don't care.
At half past two I wake up my mum,
She says 'Go back to bed you are so dumb.'

I walk back to bed and my dad says I look like I'm dead.

It's Christmas day, hooray, hooray, let's start a parade.
My presents are here, I open my eyes and it is such a surprise.

I have a look, I've been so good.
I got this T-shirt with a hood.
I pick up a gift, it's a garage with a lift.

Mark Searle (11)
Blaise Primary School

CHRISTMAS DAY

Christmas is here, I'd better get up
Oh no it's half past two.
My mum will be in a strop.
Yes, it's time, I'll run down stairs
And under the tree
There's my presents, yippee

I play on the floor then
There's a knock at the door, oh no!
It's my nan, run and hide
Under the bed.

My nan found me oh no!
Not my face, I feel sick
Stay away, let me go back
To bed.

John Roberts (11)
Blaise Primary School

THE NIGHT OF THE MOON

The night that is bright
The light of the moon
Above the clouds ever so fluffy and white.
A shooting star is what I see
It dazzles and dances right down to me.
The birds are in flight.
The stars sparkle in the night,
Glitter and gleam right on the stream
Up above so fluffy and white
Sleeps the night.

Gerard Bligh (9)
Blaise Primary School

BULLYING

In the corner of the playground
I stand all alone, I hear people whispering about me.

When we pick teams to play games
I always seem to be picked last.

In the classroom nobody sits by me
I try to sit by people but they just move away.

In the dinner hall I'm always the very last to get my dinner
And when I sit down next to someone they move away.

Oh why, oh why can't I have a friend even for one day?
Please let me have a friend.

Christopher Chinn (11)
Blaise Primary School

MOONLIGHT

The moon is so bright
It shines every night
It sparkles and it makes me happy.
And the next day it's as sparkly as yesterday.

I like it when it's bright at night
He loves it at night
I sing to the moon
And the moon sings back to me.

The moon is so round
It makes a lovely sound
It's so silver and really it is such a sight.

Chloe Parnell (9)
Blaise Primary School

THE MAGIC MOON

The moon is bright
The moon is big
What's that I hear?
A falling twig.
I look out my window
And what do I see?
A badger and hedgehog
Staring at me.
The stars are bright
The moon is green
It is the biggest thing
I have ever seen.
The stars are bright
The birds in flight
Amongst the clouds
All fluffy and white.
The silvery sky is a
Magnificent sight.
I wish I was high
Right up in the sky
To watch the magnificent
World go by.

Daniel Saunders (10)
Blaise Primary School

FRIENDSHIP

A friend is always there
When nobody else will care.
Caring and sharing through good and bad
Even when times are sad.

Friendship is fine all the time
My friends are fine.
It's lovely when we're sharing
My friend is very caring.

Rochelle Bowman (10)
Blaise Primary School

THE FIGHT

I hit his head
He pulled my leg
He twisted my arm
I shouted in alarm
He kicked my shin
I stabbed him with a pin,

Then suddenly we made friends
We thought it was best
And now we're more than friends
We're better than the rest.

Ross Jeakings (9)
Blaise Primary School

THE MOON POEM

The moon is white
The moon is cold, dark and gloomy
The moon, the moon in the sky
I can see the big round moon.

Michelle Betteridge (9)
Blaise Primary School

DRUGS ARE REALLY STUPID THINGS TO TAKE

Drugs are really stupid things to take, they damage your head,
Stop taking those things.

Drugs can ruin your family,
You can hallucinate that big frogs are coming to get you,
Stop taking these things.

Drugs can kill you very slowly and you don't know.
It can also damage your kidneys and your liver,
Stop taking these things.

They hook you on them but they don't take you off,
They sell their drugs like they just don't care,
Stop taking these things.

They come in pills and all sorts of things like tattoos,
Stop taking these things.

Whoever takes these sort of things are just fools
And you can die just like that,
So stop taking these drugs.

Stephanie Farrell (10)
Blaise Primary School

FRIENDSHIP

Friends are there for you when you need them.
Here and there, everywhere, sing a song,
Be happy together, and stay with each other,
Trust each other.
Don't forget the sharing part!
It's lovely to share so come on everybody
Be happy and let's all be friends.

Kathryn Winson (9)
Blaise Primary School

MRS FRY

Mrs Fry is our headteacher
And she's very nice if you go to meet her.

But if you go with something bad
She'll sit and stare
Then she'll shout and swear!

But if you go with something good
She'll feel very proud
And say 'Well done Lee, you've found the key.'

Mrs Fry is our headteacher
And she's *very nice* when you go to meet her.

Rebecca Watkin (10) & Laura Williamson (10)
Blaise Primary School

FRIENDSHIP

A friend can make you smile
He's someone who really cares
When things go wrong he'll stay a while,
His time and feelings he always shares.

I've got a very nice friend
Who is very kind
Our friendship will never come to an end
But if it does I won't mind.

Liam Harper (10) & Ashley Winnett (9)
Blaise Primary School

I LIKE THE MOON

I like the moon
it's sparkly, shiny and beautiful.
Sometimes the moon is full,
so don't be a fool!
The moon blazed
in my bedroom, so it's bright.

I like the moon.

Stephen Phillips (9)
Blaise Primary School

THE SOLAR SYSTEM

Planets.
Neptune and Mars.
The Sun, Venus, Earth too.
They're all in the solar system.
It's big!

Amy Potter (10)
Blaise Primary School

SHINES LIKE A LIGHT

The moon is bright
it shines like a light.
In the dark and deepest water
it makes the water glittery
and hides behind the clouds.
It always comes out at night
but sadly goes down.

Mehul Pandit (9)
Blaise Primary School

THE SPARKLY MOON

The moon moves slowly and silently.
The bright light shines at night.
The trees' branches look silver in the moon.
And things like sounds go boom.

The moon always smiles
The moon shines for miles and miles.

And the loony tunes
Visit the moon and
Every night with light.

The moon is very, very bright.

Michelle Davies (9)
Blaise Primary School

FRIENDSHIP

Friends bring happiness
just by being there.
The magic of a friend
is that they'll always share.

Friends always care
through joy and sorrow.
You will see your friends
yesterday, today and tomorrow.

Danielle Fletcher (9)
Blaise Primary School

FRIENDSHIP

It's nice to share with a friend.
When you are happy the day will never end.
We are all nice and kind
Our friendship is covered with all our mind.

Then I am alone a friend is never there.
I like a friend around me showing that they care.
I like friends around me.
We always have a good time and especially at tea.

Leanne Pavloff (9)
Blaise Primary School

MOONLIGHT

I look out my window
And what do I see?
Some feathers as bright as can be
It sparkles, it shines,
It opens the blinds,
And shines and shines.

Michael Baker (8)
Blaise Primary School

THE BRIGHT MOON

The moon is light
The moon is bright
The moon shines down every night
The moon sparkles on the roofs
And never goes down.
My sparkling moon.

Danielle Roseway (8)
Blaise Primary School

HAPPINESS

Happiness starts with a smile
Then when you least expect it to
It comes right back to you.
Through your life it goes,
Making happiness show.
Making your life a good one.
Making it better for everyone.

Nicky Townsend (9)
Blaise Primary School

GOLDEN, SILVER

The dazzling moonlit sky
that's glistening bright and high
with silky, golden night air mist
flowing round my ankles in a twist.
Silver light dances on cobblestones,
moonlight bright to guide me home.

Nikki Smith (10)
Blaise Primary School

A MAGICAL MOON

It's light
It's bright
It's a big delight
Craters and holes
It's a magical night
It glows and gleams all bright and light
Oh what a big fright
All in the night.

Daniel Rankin (9)
Blaise Primary School

MOONLIGHT

When I see the moon at night,
Floating with a shimmery light.
I feel some magic in the air,
I just want to sit and stare.
The moon is very, very bright.

The moon shines on every tree,
Twinkles on every owl and glistens on me.
The moon leaves a silvery trail,
I think it's a bit like a snail.
The moon is very, very bright.

When the moon rises it could be full,
Or it could be like the horn of a bull.
Part black, part white, is the moon
It will be dawn soon.
The moon won't be very, very bright.

Rebecca Varker (8)
Blaise Primary School

A FRIEND IS THERE

Wherever you are
Whatever you do
A friend is always
There for you.

Whenever you're hurt
Whenever you're not
A friend is there for
You in a little dot.

Jake Smith (8)
Blaise Primary School

THE MOON SHINES

Moonlight shines upon the night
Overjoyed, the moon shines bright.

Gleaming as the moon turns round,
Not making a single sound.

Cold and bright in the night
Making everything go very bright.

Victoria Kendall (10)
Blaise Primary School

THE SOLAR SYSTEM

Planets
Pluto and Mars
Are my favourites,
They are both near all the other ones.
That's cool!

Komal Pandit (10)
Blaise Primary School

THE SILVERY MOON

The silvery moon shines on the sea
It lights up a patch for you and me.
It shines brightly in the night
And over the land it spreads its light.
The moon controls the turning tides
And when the daybreak comes it hides.
Until the dark and glittery night
When it shines again all fresh and bright.

Louisa Jones (9)
Blaise Primary School

THE BARE MOON

The moon is light,
The moon is bright,
It shivers up there,
Cold and bare.
Sometimes I like to stand and stare,
As I watch it in bed at night,
It seems so very, very bright.
As I drift off to sleep,
I just give a last little peep.

Joe Clarke (9)
Blaise Primary School

BLUE SEA

Water
Is good for you.
It is in the blue sea.
It is very healthy for you.
It's cold.

Ben Stephens (12)
Blaise Primary School

THE SPARKLY MOON

The moon is bright
The moon is sparkly
The moon shines up
It never goes down
The moon sparkles over the sea
The moon is magical as can be.

Katie-Jane Searle (8)
Blaise Primary School

THE MOON

M oving
O ver hilltops, moving through the sky, moving
O ver houses, making them clear to see.
N ow it's on another street
L ighting up the houses as
I t moves through the sky
G oing to different places
H ere it is now peeping
T hrough the clouds, bringing a new day to us.

Stacey Cawley (9)
Blaise Primary School

RUN!

Run far.
Run for your life
Run away and hide.
Run now, for the good of mankind.
Just run!

George Archdeacon-Turner (11)
Blaise Primary School

GLISTENING MOON

As the moon sits and smiles
it shines over for miles and miles.
As it shines down at night
large and round glistening so bright.
As it peers from the clouds
it still shines on like chandeliers.

Nicola Mitchelmore (10)
Blaise Primary School

SILVER

Silver wind goes past the silver trees.
Moonlit candles go round the moon
And sparkles on the silver seas.
This and that it glows upon the trees.
Silver birds fly up so high
And go down like a silver fly.

David Bundy (9)
Blaise Primary School

BLOODTHIRSTY FANGS

Sharp teeth.
Sharp cut-throat claws,
Long stripy swaying tail.
You'd better watch out man-eaters.
Killers!

Warren Rumsey (11)
Blaise Primary School

THE BIG OCEAN

It's deep and it's cold, it moves around,
It's blue and wavy, it's the sea,
It hops like a flea.

Sundee Spaulding (11)
Blaise Primary School

THE EXCITING JOURNEY

It's wide,
It's enormous,
It flows and waves calmly.
It goes on exciting journeys.
Water!

Zoe Sanders (11)
Blaise Primary School

KEEP BACK

Keep back
From the ocean.
It's big and takes you down.
It throws you about and then you drown.
Keep back!

David Holbrook (11)
Blaise Primary School

ICEBERGS

Icebergs
Are dangerous.
Rock solid icebergs.
The Atlantic Ocean is full of them.
Dangerous!

Matthew Wilmott (11)
Blaise Primary School

THE SILVER MOON

The moon is silver.
It walks in its
silver shoon.
Some people say
the moon's made of
cheese.
I think they're
mad or if they're
not mad
they must have
gone batty for
the moon is not
made of cheese.
I look out of
my window, the
moon is as
bright as can be.
I heard
a noise, I look
into the garden.
I see a fox
run across the
garden . . .
Then I go to
bed
but I hear
a noise again.

It was just my
hamster in his
wheel so there's
nothing to worry
about!
The moon is silver.

Steven Barnett (9)
Blaise Primary School

COLOURS

What is green?
Green is the wet grass in a field.

What is red?
Red is a juicy apple.

What is blue?
Blue is the sparkling sea.

What is yellow?
Yellow is a buttercup in a field.

What is orange?
An orange of course!

Curtis Reid (8)
Blaise Primary School

BLOOD

Blood's red.
Blood is not nice.
Blood flows out when you're hurt.
Vampires also like drinking blood.
Watch out!

Annie Jordan (10)
Blaise Primary School

THE TWO TYPES OF CATS

There are two types of cats, you understand,
Let us firstly consider the Sleepy type of puss;

Lazing about all day, dreaming in the sun,
Sleeping on the window-sill, drowsing on the bed,
Lazing in the sunshine, dreaming all the day.

This type of cat can be considered to be a Heatsink.

Let us now consider the Energetic kind of puss;
Running round all day, - Hereandtheireian,
Inandoutian, Toandfroian, Waltzingroundian,
Onthebedian sort of cat.

There is an overlap between the two.
Therefore the bed may be considered to be the
                    natural habitat of the cat.

My bed, that is.

Kendall Atcliffe (9)
Callicroft Junior School

FAIRIES

Down the garden
a feint little light
but it wasn't that bright.
It lead me to it
I go to touch it
but then it jumped away.
I thought I knew what it was.
it had to be a fairy
and it was.
Then it jumped into my hand
and shouted its name 'Anabell.'
Then disappeared.
I will always remember
that bright spring morning
when I saw a fairy.

Carly Cockram (11)
Callicroft Junior School

THE WOODS

As I look out of this window, I see 'the woods'.
Cold air passes through their grey branches as they hold on to the sky.
Mist clings to their trunks, it seems as though their trunks have faces.
The faces stare at me, with deep grey features.
As I look away from this window, I see the book I write on.

Robert Flitter (11)
Callicroft Junior School

SPACE

First I see a dark black bleakness,
Stretching as far as I can see,
Silence I also hear.
Then I hear faint tingling noises,
They were stars.
Hundreds and hundreds of silver stars,
Like a crowd of fire-flies.
Then right before me in front of my eyes
I see a giant ball,
It was like a ball of fire.
But no it was the sun.
My next visit was the planets.
First Mars.
The big red ball, the sign of danger.
Next Venus.
The turquoise colour, the planet that sucks you
And squashes you.
Then Jupiter.
Big, round, the colour of dawn.
Finally Pluto.
The small, blue planet, blue as coldness.
Then back home,
Through the galaxy of fire-flies,
The stars.

Stephanie Wrench (11)
Callicroft Junior School

MY FRIENDS IN THE SKY

The stars in the sky,
like glitter in the night,
they shine,
they twinkle,
they blink.

Looking down on me,
they are my friends,
they make me feel safe,
when I sleep.

Kurt Ratnett (7)
Callicroft Junior School

SCHOOL BULLIES

I'm a rough school bully,
I don't bother to learn,
What I do all day is
Watch telly, fight and chearn.

I've a book about wrestling,
But I don't know how to read!
My mum said 'You should join first aid'
In case I start to bleed.

I'm a rough school bully,
I almost always eat,
And last week when I did PE
I got splinters in my feet.

I hate school dinners,
They always make me sick,
All they have for pudding,
Is fruit and spotted dick.

I'm a rough school bully,
Now my teacher's never to frown,
Because my dad has told her,
I'm finally leaving town.

James Gordon (8)
Callicroft Junior School

THE CREEPY HOUSE

I once went to a creepy house,
It had spiders, and millions of bats,
I even got a fever once,
It might have been the rats.

I liked it in the creepy house,
Although I get scared to death,
I try to move away quite fast,
Before I take a breath.

Maybe if I take breath
It may just stop the noise,
But I am very scared you know
So I shall call the boys.

Adam James (8)
Callicroft Junior School

THE HAUNTED HOUSE

There is a house upon the hill,
that everyone fears is haunted.
I wanted to sleep up there just to prove them wrong.
They said it was unsafe, I suppose I should have listened.
I said I was not scared and I trudged on up there,
I got in the house and a mouse was sat on the chair,
I thought it was safe but it turned out a disgrace.
The window opened and then slammed shut,
I thought this was it and I had a fit,
and ran humiliated down the hill.

Charlotte Toleman (10)
Callicroft Junior School

IN THE BARN

One day in the barn
Sitting in the hay
I found an baby alien
He didn't run away
I asked him what his name was
He said he didn't know
I said I'd make one up for him
'I think I'll call you Glow.'
I took Glow to my den
And sat him on the floor
He said in a funny accent
'Can I call you Bloor?'
I said 'Very well, then'
Because I didn't mind
Then Glow leapt, he ran away
And left me far behind.

Kayleigh Griffiths (8)
Callicroft Junior School

THE ORANGE SHADOW

King of the beasts,
Moves silently through the African plain,
Relies on his speed and cunning mind,
Stands tall and straight with his furry mane,
Hear his roar see his teeth,
Don't try to outwit this powerful beast,
Ready to run,
Ready to pounce,
Ready to kill,
Ready to eat,
Zebra doomed.

Edward Waymouth (11)
Chandag Junior School

THE UNKNOWN CREATURE

Quiet
silence
throughout the
ocean
swiftly gliding
through smooth
waters
proud, brave
alert and curious
exploring the unknown
world
searching for his next
meal
with hungry eyes
pointed strong dagger
teeth
He is the king of the ocean
The great white
Shark!

Rachel Harbour (8)
Chandag Junior School

HOMELESS

Dirty, poor, alone, homeless,
Sick of all the staring.
Those greedy people,
Never think of sharing.

Why they don't,
I do not know.
They're always like it,
No love to show.

This place, so cold,
I wish I was warm.
These people with money
Sometimes I wish I wasn't born.

I might give up,
I've got no hope,
It's really sad,
How can I cope?

Patrick Nazemi (10)
Chandag Junior School

BUTTERFLY

Flutters,
Softly,
With elegance,
Soundless,
Silent.
That's what he is;
Gentle and small.
His patterned wings,
Perfect,
Gliding through the sky.
Dainty,
Shy,
Stands out in a big blue sky.
With bliss he moves,
And with style,
Just drifting,
Drifting.

Andrew Griffiths (11)
Chandag Junior School

ME ON THE ROADSIDE

Me under a shelter
Searching through a bin.
Banging on doors
Shouting 'Let me in.'

Me on the roadside
Cold and bare
All people do is
Stop and stare.

I'm on the pavement
No one to care
No one to love
And no one to share.

Leanne Cains (10)
Chandag Junior School

BUTTERFLIES

Small and swift
Neatly turning and twisting
Elegant and soft
Gently gliding and swaying
All colours in the air
It flutters by in the sky
No one knows where it goes
Prettier than all
Amazing colours like reds, greens and blues
Prettiest animal in the world
Some are camouflaged
Some are bright
Gone!

Oliver Neech (11)
Chandag Junior School

WILD CREATURE

Swinging into action
leaping through the wild jungle
darting for his life
sprinting flashes in the sun
fear is approaching
this wild creature
heart beating thumping
birds flutter
danger looks upon this poor old
face of the creature
he looks round
dripping fangs.

Aaron Ward (10)
Chandag Junior School

IT'S A FROG'S LIFE

Croak! Croak! Croak!
It belongs in a lake full of teeming life
Where it captures gnats
With its long and gummy tongue.
It bounds with energy as it bounces
From lily to lily.
Its complexion is murky green,
So it hides away then spots its prey
Then vaults out and eats it with joy.
Its boggly eyes are the size of marbles
And as clear as the sky above
All the better to observe its food
Before he gobbles it up.
Yum! Yum!

Sarah Baxter (11)
Chandag Junior School

SNOW

White emulsion drifts down,
Covering everything.
Trees to ghosts,
More freezing emulsion drifts
To the ground,
Turning the school white.
Snowballs soar through the
Atmosphere,
As a white blanket develops.
You put out your tongue,
Catch some magic emulsion
Drifting down,
Arctic water,
In your tummy,
School embarks,
Playtime comes,
Children wail,
As the teacher forbids us to go out,
Into a sea of white paint.

Matthew Dyson (9)
Chandag Junior School

IF I COULD NOT SEE

If I could not see where would I be?
No trees, no water, flowers or birds.
What would I think? What would I do?
Not able to play football, cricket or tennis.
If I could not see I wouldn't know what
Blue, yellow, pink or red was like.
So I must think how lucky I am to see.

Michael Davis (9)
Chandag Junior School

FOX IN FLIGHT

Crunch, snap, rustle
    feet pattering across the leafy ground
Bubbling of a stream,
        singing of the birds
A whirl of glowing ginger
    sweeping past me,
crunch, crunch fills the air
    scampering feet getting faster
Ginger white front feet spread out.
    The back legs spring in slow motion up in the air
        Bushy tail upright for balance
    Sprinting past me twisting and turning
In the burning sun never ending corners like a maze.
    Owl hooting, humans shooting
        scampering over twigs
Heart beating rapidly, diving through bushes
        stop still
Birds start to sing,
        owl stops hooting
    humans stop shooting
walks swiftly, silently to its den
    The forest has turned to spring with a humming
in the air and a cool, gentle breeze
        as the sun sets in the pink and orange sky.

Kerry Mawby (10)
Chandag Junior School

ESCAPE OF THE FOREST FOX

Leaping through the air,
Its powerful hind legs pushing with an
Incredible force of power.
A blur of fiery red overcoat.
Eyes glowing, whiskers twitching.
With beautiful grace the fox landed.
Quick as a flash it was off.
Off into the maze of tall green trees.
It stopped, ears pricked.
Rustle, rustle, rustle.
A squirrel, giving the fox a warning.
      Hunters!
Speeding through the cool wet forest,
Hardly any light,
Heart pounding,
Tail swishing,
Eyes glowing.
Red, slender body makes it easy to dodge trees.
Home at last,
Safe from the predator,
Just escaped death.

Anna Leese (10)
Chandag Junior School

HOW LUCKY I AM TO SEE

Look at the blue of sky,
The green grass in the meadow,
The gold in the sun,
The twinkle in the child's eye.
I must think how lucky I am to see,
The beauty of the world around me.

Sarah Godsland (9)
Chandag Junior School

THE SLY SHADOW

Light gone
Moon shining,
Eyes glinting,
Running quickly, slickly, slyly,
Hungrily scavenging through dustbins,
Her golden red coat turning mucky,
Leaving trails of destruction.
Vixen's her name, cubs soon expected
So rush to her earth,
Sewer or park.

Cubs now here,
Give a muffled sort of whine,
Food they say,
Vixen goes,
Already on a little mouse's trail,
Pounces high,
Got it
Go
Nibbling berries on the way.

Cubs now give a contented groan,
Gnawing sightlessly on their food,
Sun is rising
Go to bed
Most repeats tomorrow
But now go to your cosy divan,
Cubs wrapped up in their mother's brush.

Jayne Hillier (11)
Chandag Junior School

WHERE DID THEY ALL GO?

They disappeared
Went away
Deserted me
On this very day

Defying death
Day after day
A life full of fear
Is there no other way?

I have no home
Just this street
No family to care
No friends to meet

Darkness comes in
I try to sleep
But all I hear is
An alarm beep

I wonder why
They all stare
It seems like
Nobody cares.

Henry Thorpe (9)
Chandag Junior School

THE STORM

Dark clouds overhead,
Sweeping from the east,
Clouds hovering over trees,
Like curtains closing, blocking the light.

The wind creeps in, trees sway and bend,
Wheat trembles with fear,
Clouds thicken in the gathering gloom,
When will the storm appear?

Joanna Humphries & Lucie Bartlett (10)
Chandag Junior School

SNOW!

I step into the garden,
White and fluffy,
A blanket of nothingness,
The curtain of white crushes under my feet,
I step deeper into it,
Pom-pom balls float down on me,
Melting on my tongue,
Blotting out my prints,
An artist of frost.

My house coated in a curtain,
White chimneys sticking out,
I touch the paint,
Powdery,
Wet,
Cool,
Lovely,
Brilliant,
All is soundless,
All is white.

All sound muffles,
A faraway friend.

Daniel Buttar (8)
Chandag Junior School

SNOW

Woke one morning
To find
Jack Frost had splashed
The whole place white
During the night!
Far away,
People skate on frozen lakes.
Couldn't wait and,
Quick as a flash,
Ran downstairs,
Went outside,
Faintly heard creaking skates.
Snow cold as ice-cream,
Stepping closer into the white sheet,
Feels crunchy under feet,
Smelling dampness from trees,
Fluffy marshmallows where apples used to be.
Snowball fights,
Another white carpet falling from buckets,
Covering the land once more.
Tastes ice cold,
Snowflakes falling,
Looking like whipped cream,
Feeling soft as feathers,
Covering the land,
Go back inside,
Cuddle up,

No need to freeze like an iceberg,
Watching snow slowly melt,
Changing into nothingness,
Leaving behind
All that was
Before.

Nicola Trout (9)
Chandag Junior School

SNOWY DAY

Open the curtains
What do you see?
But a blanket all over the place.
Everything covered and hidden away.
Rush downstairs
Great!
Smelling fresh as countryside,
A silent atmosphere outside.
Drifting down from above
Bits of mashed potato
Like elegant little flakes,
Making little crunches as you step.
Children coming out to play,
Gleaming white thrown across the sky,
Snow people develop in back gardens,
Vanilla ice-cream on the land,
You could just eat it,
But don't stand out there and freeze
Like an ice block in a freezer.

Ashley Percival (9)
Chandag Junior School

A WHITE NOTHINGNESS

At night
Dark, gloomy
But outside a demon came
Plastering everything white.
It came down twisting, twirling, whirling
The movements of a ballet dancer.
I woke up, glanced out
Nothing was heard
Apart from my heavy breath
Nothing was seen
But everything was whitewashed clean.
I got on my wellies
Put on my coat
Rushed outside like a tornado.
Ground saturated by snow.
Started to plod
Made noises like crisps
Tastes like vanilla ice-cream
Soothing down my throat.
Sheet of white nothingness
Concealing the land.
Icicles started emerging on my nose
A touch of warm sunlight made
A cold icy demon die.

Martin Clarke (9)
Chandag Junior School

RAINY DAYS

Rainy days are boring,
I usually stay in bed.
I hear raindrops
Dropping off the roof
Plop
And crash into a thousand pieces.
I really want to go outside
Into the mushy puddles.
Climb into my bright red wellingtons
And pull on my woolly coat.
Why do adults make a fuss?
I like to play
Not miss the rain
Which comes again and again.

Heather Baker (9)
Chandag Junior School

SNOW WONDERLAND

I awake to find snow everywhere
I grab my coat, scarf, woolly hat, gloves.
Snow drifting, floating down.
Layering blankets,
Thick like quilts.
Looks like vast, feathery, fluffy clouds.
Sounds like constant nothingness.
Deadens, softens, stifles the air.
Tastes like soft, fluffy, whipped cream.
Feels like ice-cream, soft and smooth.

Laura Hubbard (9)
Chandag Junior School

SNOW

When I unfastened the curtain
What did I see?
Snow everywhere
Covering the landscape like a sheet of paper.
Picking some up it felt crispy,
Crispy and cold
Tasting like vanilla ice-cream.
Fluffy, puffy clouds everywhere
Plop, plop on lakes, streams
Like white paint
Painting all things surrounding me.
Trees looking like ghosts,
Scary shadows on the earth.
Then the sun approaches
Melting the snow
Like melted chocolate on a hot day.

Ben Parkinson-King (8)
Chandag Junior School

THE DESERT

The hot, exposed desert,
Not a cloud in the sky,
A yellow moonscape
As far as the eye can see
Parched and lifeless,
Cactus,
Scattered like land mines,
A wild, barren space,
No vehicles travel here
For this is the graveyard.

Louise Evans, Ben Israel & Richard Skuse (10)
Chandag Junior School

SNOW

Oh snow, how bitter and cold you are,
You came at night and varnished it white,
Why can't you come another time?
You're fluffy white candyfloss
But crunchy white and plain.
Oh I wish you wouldn't come
With all your mustard icy white!
I wish the sun would come and turn you yellow.
But the sun can't come in December
Next time come in November!

You float so lightly,
But tumble if you're not careful,
Then when you hit the ground you transform into tiny solid squares.
Then after a while you break and drift away.
So snow, why do you take so long when you stay?
When I lay in bed that night I heard a crackle and a bang.
I looked out of the window last night.
Oh joy you've gone, you've gone!
The snow has gone away.

Virginia Golf (8)
Chandag Junior School

DOLPHINS

Dolphins swimming, splashing, communicating,
Smooth, thin grey dolphins.
Plopping, laughing, flapping, gliding, reflecting.
Their bodies ripple, through the deep blue sea.
Dolphins searching for friends;
Bubbly water squirting from their soft holes.

Oliver Cartledge (8)
Chandag Junior School

SNOW

The snow drifts from the sky
Like a nice, creamy pie.
We all wake up seeing snow
In the sky
Quickly, put fluffy coats on.
Go out to play,
Making things in cold winter snow.
It looks like a sheet of white paper,
Falls like little icy petals
White trees in gardens
No flowers
They're covered with fluffy snow.

Mikaela Parker-Brown (8)
Chandag Junior School

SNOWY NIGHT

Pitter, patter through the night,
Fields, everything, gleaming white.
Sticky marshmallows coating trees,
Squishy flakes but no leaves.
Ponds, rivers, all beautiful and white,
Oh, the morning is so pleasant and bright.
Crunchy snow, freezing cold,
Oh, I love the painter who painted this snow.

Nick Walters (9)
Chandag Junior School

SNOW

The snow sounds like crisps
Crunching together.
The painter comes,
Quick!
Let's have a taste
Of the vanilla ice-cream!
It looks like mashed potato.
Dad went to work
But not in a red car,
In a white car!
Getting cold,
Let's go in.
Sitting by the fire
With a hot chocolate
And a cookie.
Goodbye painter,
Will you come back tomorrow?

Hannah Riddoch (9)
Chandag Junior School

KING OF THE FISH

Silence
in the deep, dark, muddy ocean.
Searching for its next meal.
Gliding proudly with his hungry eyes,
teeth as sharp and pointed as axes
exploring the unknown.
Lord of the ocean
is the great white shark.

Jessica Tulit (8)
Chandag Junior School

THE OCEAN DANGERS

Silence
Through the murky oceans.
Swimming gracefully like a bird.
Alert for dangers.
Waiting for his prey.
Proud, brave,
The predator
Teeth like a dagger
He is the beast

The great white
Shark!

Fiona Mackenzie (8)
Chandag Junior School

KING OF THE OCEAN

Silence!
In the deep, dark, murky ocean
with teeth as sharp as a knife,
huge, proud, brave
gliding swiftly through silky waters,
exploring the unknown murky world
unbeatable,
invincible.
The great white shark.

Ian Bodman (7)
Chandag Junior School

RAINDROPS

The rain has paused.
The sun comes out
Droplets hang,
Or spread about.
On spindly stems.
On grasses and leaves.
On cobwebs, petals,
And gathered in sheaves.

The clear raindrops
Like little gems,
Hang in line
Along the stems,
Bending it over
Weighing it down,
Touching the grass
Like a jewelled crown.

Ben Farler & Emma Quinn (10)
Chandag Junior School

KING OF THE OCEAN

In the depths of deep, dark, murky sea waters,
Something moves swiftly on the ocean floor,
Its eyes hunting for the next meal,
Proudly moving into an unknown world,
Still hunting for his prey,
Feeling lost and lonely as he travels through the seas.
Huge fins flapping as he moves
Gracefully like a flying bird.

Scarlett Potticary (7)
Chandag Junior School

DESERT

Scorching sand,
Blistering feet,
Travelling miles,
For many a week,
Lizard burrowing into the ground,
Desert squirrels leaping around,
All to escape the heat.

Ships of the desert,
Sail over the sand,
How do they survive,
In this wilderness land?
Sidewinders moving quickly around,
With only two points touching the ground,
All to escape the heat.

Night comes in,
Temperatures fall,
Sandstorms a threat,
The wind starts to squall,
The sand is tossed,
The dunes are lost.
No need to escape the heat.

Harrison Smith, Emma Geen & Sarah Leybourne (10)
Chandag Junior School

THREE DOLPHINS

Three little dolphins swimming in the sea,
can you count them, one, two, three?
Two little dolphins swimming in the ocean blue,
can you count them, none, one, two?

Those two dolphins,
go on through the sea.
The one that left comes back again,
then there are three.

Michael Arnold (8)
Chandag Junior School

DOLPHINS EVERYWHERE

Dolphins, dolphins everywhere.
Communicating clicks as they
Swim in a light blue sea.
Playing happily in the water,
Playing with everything they see.

Graham Sage (7)
Chandag Junior School

DOLPHINS PLAY

Dolphins play,
Dolphins squeak,
Dolphins swim.

Swimming, squeaking, playing dolphins.

Dolphins click,
Dolphins tutt,
Dolphins cry.

Crying, clicking, tutting dolphins.

Daniel Forsyth-Skuse (7)
Chandag Junior School

SNOW

Snow gleaming, resplendent, bright, white.
Conceals, obscures, like a blanket.
Tumbling, swirling, from grey skies.
Tastes of ice-cream, creamy and sweet.
Looks like a pure white icicle.
Trails of footsteps by the garden gate.
Frozen, shivery, bitterly cold.
Sounds of crunchy cornflakes
Being munched in your mouth.
Smells of water from the tap.
I go outside,
Exploring.
Everything enveloped in white.
Freezing, chilly, still snowing.
Feels like a slimy, wet frog.
Looks like a summer's drink with lots of ice.
People having snowball fights with fuzzy balls.
It stops snowing.
My world of whiteness
All goes away.

Lucy Miles (9)
Chandag Junior School

COMMUNICATING DOLPHINS

Dolphins smooth and grey,
Dolphins in the big blue sea,
Communicating loud and clear,
They swim here, there and everywhere.
Hear their laughter in the air,
Crying, whispering dolphins.

Kirsty Baker (7)
Chandag Junior School

THE BIRTH AND DEATH OF SIN

When it is born
it is like a knife blade stabbing at
your soul,
It tears at your insides,
Eating away all traces of light,
Trying to drag you into the bowels
of hell,
Torturing you night and day and
sacrificing good for evil,
But when it dies it is like a touch of
pleasure,
Your first taste of heaven,
The linen enveloped mummy returns
again to rest peacefully in its tomb,
The black clouds disperse from your
mind.

Simon Pearce (10)
Chew Stoke CE Primary School

THE VOID

Darkness crept on them like a tiger hunting its prey;
Hiding all day,
Waiting for the right time,
Like death.
As the shadows grew they looked like someone twisting, mutating.
Slowly turning to void.
Light came like a saviour from the black and twisted shadows,
The light demolished the void like a mist devouring bad and evil.

Matthew Cole (10)
Chew Stoke CE Primary School

THE SECRET WEAPON

It's like black clouds swarming over me,
Telling me they will never leave,
Telling me what terrible torture they have in store,
I don't know what to do,
I am lost in confusion,
My conscience is thumping my head,
I open my mouth,
I open my mouth and let the secret weapon pour out,
This weapon is *sorry,*
The relief is like a snake finally shedding its skin,
Now I know *sorry* is the true weapon,
I am free.

Fee Pearce (10)
Chew Stoke CE Primary School

THE LEOPARD'S HUNT

The hunter was out,
His eyes were on me,
It was like a yawning lion,
With his teeth as sharp as daggers.
He moved like the swift wind,
But as I forgave the person,
The leopard turned into a baby kitten,
With small paws and harmless teeth,
And I felt like a new man.

BenVowles (11)
Chew Stoke CE Primary School

Dinosaurs Haiku

Heavy, lumbering.
Dead for millions of years.
Killed by the Ice Age.

Scott Davies (9)
Cutlers Brook Junior School

Rugby Haiku

Head down, scrum, safe, strong.
Quick running, touch down to score.
We've won, roll in mud.

Theo Welsh (9)
Cutlers Brook Junior School

My Bedroom

My bedroom has shadows all over the wall.
When the light fades away.
I jump on my bed and hide,
Until the ghosts go away.

Helen Bourton (10)
Cutlers Brook Junior School

My Mum

Her black, shiny hair,
tied in a plait down her back,
swings when she walks fast.

Tanveer Hussain (9)
Cutlers Brook Junior School

ALONE IN THE DARK

Turn the light off, I feel scared.
My teddy's alive, I'm sure I heard it growl.
Bats in the dark, waiting to bite my neck.
That knot looks like a spider.
Eyes of a witch's cat stare at me.
Under the covers.
Noises like aliens waiting to invade.
Look out of the windows, everything's dead.
Turn the light on, my friends are back, the spooks are gone.

Roxanne Brennan (9)
Cutlers Brook Junior School

THE PARK IS VERY DARK

The park is very dark,
it's really spooky,
look there's a spark.
What is it? I start to tremble and fidget,
chattering my teeth, biting my nails.
The lights start to flash,
I want to dash,
I hear a *clink-clang*.
The park is very dark,
so beware, it's very stark.

Rachel Anderson (10)
Cutlers Brook Junior School

SCARY CAT

Is it my cat or a monster that
makes my aeroplane hook spin and
look like a spider?

Is it my cat or a monster that
sits at the bottom of my bed with
glowing eyes?

Is it my cat or a monster that
tries to climb on my bed when I'm
asleep?

That's it, I'm going to catch that
monster with a net, tonight I'll
lay in bed waiting for it.

Crrreeeaaak! He's here, as I let go
of the rope I see four eyes not two.

I drop the net, yes, he's trapped,
I tie up the other end of the net,
there's a hole in the floor, I
throw the net, it disappears
the hole closes up and disappears
too, I'll never see the monster again.

Patrick Jenkins (10)
Cutlers Brook Junior School

I'M SEEING THINGS

I think there're monsters under my bed.
A ghost opening and shutting the door.
I am scared, should I call my mum?
Under my blanket with my teddy I hide.
I peek under my bed,
Nothing there.
I sit up,
I turn on the light.
Phew! Everything back to normal.

Hanna Boyd (10)
Cutlers Brook Junior School

ALIENS

Aliens short
Aliens tall
I wonder if there are Aliens at all.
Their little ships whizzing through space,
I wonder if they might be having a race?
Alien dogs
Alien cats
Maybe they have Alien rats?
Do they sneeze
Do they wheeze
Surely they must have Alien bees!
Aliens race round stars they also race round Mars
In their little Alien cars.

Edward Bartholomew (8)
Fairfield School

DO YOU BELIEVE IN ALIENS?

Do you believe in Aliens?
The three eyed monsters
Wandering around in their strange outfits
Why are they green?
Why can't they be purple?
They probably travel around on galaxies.
Why do they have funny hands like ET?
Why can't they have our hands?

Which planet do they live on?
Moon, Jupiter or Pluto?
If I was an Alien I would live on the Moon!
I don't understand?
Why aren't they just like us?

Sophie Perrin (8)
Fairfield School

THE MOON

The moon is big,
The moon is round.
I'm sure it's not made of cheese,
It's big and white and has strange shapes,
The shapes are funny,
Some believe there's a man on the moon,
Some think there's a bunny,
But I've told you once and now again,
I think the moon is funny.

Jennie Grene (8)
Fairfield School

THE PLANETS

The stars are twinkling
The planets are circling
Mars is red
Floating over head
Jupiter's in bed.
My toes are cold
The fire is hot
My bed is cosy
But the ground is hard as lead.
I wonder, if I touched a star
Would it be as cold as my toes are
Or would it sizzle?
Would it feel lumpy or would it feel soft?
I wonder if the planets sing like the birds
Or are they silent?

George Wrightson (8)
Fairfield School

PLANETS

Planets big planets small
Some short some tall some really tall
Jupiter's big, Pluto's small,
Mars isn't big or small,
It's just right to ride a bike
On the M5 motorway.
You jump, you reach a wonderful black stuff
And you sing,
A whole new world
A dazzling place of mankind
A whole new world.

Tom Henley (8)
Fairfield School

THE SUN

The sun is just a bright angry star,
It burns up everything in its path.
It is mean,
It is mighty,
The sun is hot and bright.
It feels like the sun wants to start a fight.
The sun's rays are its weapons,
Which are far more deadly than any gun.
Whoever starts a fight with the sun
Will never forgive themselves for what they have done.
It makes people's eyes switch off
And never switch on again.
But it also give us joy,
It gives us pleasure,
It gives us shadows;
It gives us sunlight and even day and night,
And most importantly, life!

Tim Power (8)
Fairfield School

STARS

Stars, stars blink at night,
They blink and disappear when
            they think they are right.
In the morning they get eaten by the sun
            and they are peaceful,
They are burning very gently.
They softly rub against the clouds,
Which makes them warm.
There are so many stars,
Which say bed time!

Thomas Wright (8)
Fairfield School

ENORMOUS JUPITER

Compared to Jupiter
I am a small frightened little girl.
The whirling,
The screaming,
It's enough to kill off a horse in a second.
The size, he's truly enormous.
It's quite cold,
Being the fifth planet away
From the sun.
All his sixteen moons
Circling him like an eagle
Going round his nest at night.
If you were with me
You would feel the rocky lumpy surface,
Of this great planet.
I wonder if I can see Earth from here.

Caroline Organ (8)
Fairfield School

SPACE

Space is full of stars shining
     And nine beautiful planets.
Mars, Jupiter, Uranus, Saturn, Venus, Mercury,
     Neptune, Pluto and Earth.
They are all poisonous planets.
     There is no life on those deadly worlds
But beautiful in their own way.
     Pluto is smallest
And Jupiter is biggest.
     Jupiter is pink, brown and orange,
Pluto is just blue but still beautiful.

Harriet Amelia Smith (8)
Fairfield School

PLANETS AND STARS

Planets don't twinkle like the stars,
Like the headlights on some cars.
If you were on Venus you'd die.
Sometimes I wonder what's in the night sky.
If I was on the moon I'd need a space suit.
Compared to our Sun, Earth's minute!
Uranus and Neptune are middle sized
If you survived on Mars I would be surprised
If there was air on the moon
Would it make your voice go squeaky?
Would it make you act all cheeky?

David Royce (8)
Fairfield School

THE ANGRY MOON

The fiery tail disappears into the scary darkness,
The rocky moon waits for his first visitors,
Not looking forward to his rude disturbance.
As a whirring sound wakes him up,
The stars stare,
The planets ponder,
The comet stops his journey round the hot sun.
The astronaut not aware of his amazed audience,
Takes his first step on the moon,
And the moon burns up his anger
And takes a great big sigh.

Grace Perrin (8)
Fairfield School

THE CIRCLE OF WEATHER

The wind is blowing,
As strong as a gale,
It feels like falling stones,
But really it's hail,
Out comes the sun,
It is still very low,
But down comes the rain,
And forms a rainbow,
It was so foggy,
Anything could get lost,
And when I peered through the window,
I saw Jack Frost,
Down comes lightning,
Before the thunder,
The thunder was noisy,
The lightning a blunder.

Peter Edwards (10)
Gracefield Preparatory School

NO EYES

I have lost my eyes,
I have no more cries,
I ask for help,
My mum and dad melt.

I wish I saw the light,
They said, 'It was very bright,'
I still needed help,
The pain I still felt.

The pain had gone,
But it still done,
I was blind,
But not in my mind!

I hoped it would go in the night,
I woke up my 'sight',
I saw a bright light,
I have my sight.

James Flanagan (10)
Gracefield Preparatory School

THE CARIBBEAN

Jamaica is where the Reggae Boyz play,
Everybody is happy and gay,
Dean Burton scores a goal,
The players surround him in a shoal.

Turn on and listen to Caribbean Radio,
When you're driving fast or slow,
Dominica is the place to go,
Get there quick or you'll miss the show.

In the Caribbean the weather's never bad,
Especially in Trinidad,
Tobago is the place to go,
With no rain, sleet or snow.

In sunny Antigua the children play,
Kicking a ball from day to day,
When the sun goes down,
It's time to leave the town,
'See you soon!'
A man shouts from under the moon.

Luke Bachhuber (10)
Gracefield Preparatory School

LIFE

What is life?
What is the use of having a wife?
To have a baby,
Bursting with life?

Space is forever,
Space is for whenever,
You feel under the weather
But whenever I look I ask,
'What is *life*?'

What is the use,
Of having a life,
It's so meaningless to
Have a life,
What is the use
Of having a life.

If man didn't exist,
War wouldn't exist,
And if cars didn't exist,
The greenhouse effect wouldn't exist.

But we cling on to life,
As if it were the
Last thing alive,
And it's in my instinct to stay alive,
Until life dies.

Jennifer L K Hawke (10)
Gracefield Preparatory School

THE WIND

I am the wind,
Coming through the air,
Though I might get binned,
I give a few a scare.

I look down on the city at the lights so bright,
I see the people run,
The lights blind me from up here,
Even with no sun.

I scurry through the lanes,
Bringing litter with me,
Although I get some pains
The litter still keeps with me.

I go where I wish,
Maybe killing people with me,
I go beneath the fish
But the fishes looks are with me.

James Blackburn (10)
Gracefield Preparatory School

FANTASY LAND

The space shuttle was very fast!
Through what we passed,
I saw Fantasy Land,
As my dog held my hand.

We landed on the shuttle line
And I was running out of time
Before I woke up from my dream
But oh Fantasy Land did gleam.

Sophie Arnold (10)
Gracefield Preparatory School

WEATHER

The rain,
Is a pain,
The wind blows the weather-vane,
And it drives you insane.

The sun is hot,
Quite a lot,
In the sky is like a yellow dot
It is as hot
As a boiling pot.

The snow is cold,
And very old,
The freezing cold,
Makes mould.

A rainbow,
Is not very low,
The hail,
Is as hard as a nail.

Timothy Sadler (11)
Gracefield Preparatory School

HARVEST

Harvest time is coming,
Fruits and crops are ripening,
It's time for a new school year,
Let's all have a cheer.

As I look for conkers,
People think I'm bonkers,
Climbing up the trees,
In the autumn breeze.

In a field I see a mouse,
Half a mile from my house,
I see a man growing crops,
So he can sell them in the shops.

We are all having fun,
Conker fights to be won,
I'm going to be at my best,
For the next harvest.

Ben Mealing (9)
Gracefield Preparatory School

WAR

I'm going off to war,
I imagine it will be sore;
I leave tomorrow,
I'll leave in sorrow.

I get given a gun,
This is not going to be fun.
I start to fight,
This is a horrible sight.

I see my flag in the sky,
It is flying high,
I see Hitler run away,
That's where he will stay.

It's the last day of war,
We are all very sore.
Hitler is dead,
He shot himself in the head.

Andrew Gunningham (11)
Gracefield Preparatory School

RIVER

I am flowing down the stream,
I can feel the beam
Of the very warm sun
And sometimes it's fun.

I am coming to the mud,
And the flower bud
Is going to come out.
Oh no! that boy is going to shout.

I'm picking up speed,
And I'm still in the lead.
I'm going over stones,
But I haven't many bones.

I am coming to the river,
And I'm going to shiver.
I'm under a bridge,
But I am also going over a ridge.

A boy is in the water ahead,
And I've just gone past a shed.
I don't like the ocean,
But someone's left their sun lotion.

Stephen Hooper (9)
Gracefield Preparatory School

MY TURKISH DELIGHT

This year we are going to Turkey,
I will eat Turkish Delights,
And I'll go to loads of parties,
And dance through all of the nights.

Turkey's a place to visit,
And not a thing to eat,
I'm sure I will enjoy it,
Despite the dangerous heat.

My brother's coming with us,
But he can be a pain,
I think we'll go to Turkey
And send him off to Spain!

Eleanor Smith (9)
Hambrook Primary School

SPRING DAY

It's a lovely spring day
When the horses neigh
And birds fly
In the sky.
Flowers are growing
Gardeners are mowing
Lambs are bleating
Cows are eating
Children's laughter fills the air
While the breeze blows through their hair.

Harriet Lamb (9)
Hambrook Primary School

MY FAVOURITE FLOWERS

They're delicate, white and dainty,
The yellow faces are pollen,
You can make chains, necklaces and bracelets,
Some people say they're weeds.
           What are they?

The trumpets are glossy and yellow,
They stand straight up tall,
They come in early spring
In pots, gardens and sometimes woods,
           What are they?

These also come in spring,
Orange, mauve, yellow and white cups,
Growing in rockeries, grass and flower beds,
Making saffron for cooking and dyeing.
           What are they?

In the meadows with the cows,
Glittering gold is the sun,
Put under your chin to see a light,
To show me if you like butter.
           What are they?

Kerina Evans (9)
Hambrook Primary School

FORMULA ONE

Formula One is fast, the season has just begun,
Today they raced in Melbourne, and it's McLaren who have won.

It looked certain that David Coulthard would win,
But he let his team mate overtake him.

Who drove the least amount of laps? I think it was Rubens Barrichello,
Oh yes, I nearly forgot Damon Hill's car is now yellow.

The bit that makes me want to eat my shoe,
Michael Schumacher's engine blew.

James Baldwin (8)
Hambrook Primary School

ON THE FARM

Down on the farm,
There is a big barn.
In the barn there is an owl,
And also a lot of chicken fowl.
One chicken has a chick
The farmhouse is made of red brick.
In the house there is a cat,
Who sits on the hearth mat.
In the lake there are some ducks.
It stinks when the farmer spreads the muck.
In the field there is a rabbit,
The fox can never, ever grab it.
There is a very, very big,
Black and white pot bellied pig.
The problem with our prize winning goose,
Is he always seems to get on the loose.
On the farm we have some cows,
And some top notch ploughs.
We have a very nice combine,
And this year crops are very fine.
The farm is really, really great,
And I have a friend my horse is my best mate.

Sebastian David Pike (10)
Hambrook Primary School

MY PERFECT DAY

My perfect day would start like this
A cuddle from my mum a kiss,
Then slowly out of bed I'd get,
Some lovely things ahead I bet.
A spot of telly, something good
Sister, Sister, Robin Hood
Fill my tummy with Coco Pops then
Off to play with Josh I'd hop.
Footie games around about, one of us
Scores, *'goal,'* we shout.
In for lunch, a special treat
Milk shake, sandwich then some sweets.
And after that a trip with dad
I really am a lucky lad.
See a film, play in the park
Don't come home until it's dark
Then, finally when it gets late
Into bed, my day's been great.

Stuart Payne (9)
Hambrook Primary School

BABY ANIMALS

A baby bobcat goes prowling for fun!
N othing is better than seeing that!
I n the water a baby dolphin plays.
M onkey babies play in trees hanging upside down.
A baby turtle has to fend for itself, unlucky isn't it?
L ovely is a new-born foal that takes its first gallop across a meadow.
S mall is a baby, pink, skinny mouse, so cute to see.

Georgina Hooper (9)
Hambrook Primary School

FAMILIES

Family is . . . what makes you strong
Because they're there for you.

When times are hard and things get rough
Your family is there for you.

When you're ill or in the blues
They're always there for you.

When you've time to spare and things to share
They're always there with you.

When you need advice or a listening ear
Is your family there for you?

Mine is!

Grace McLarty (9)
Hambrook Primary School

PARENTS

Parents are bossy,
Parents are cruel,
Parents are fussy
They make the rules.

They come in different shapes and sizes,
They treat you as their crop,
They're always mean, they're always misers,
You can't buy them in the shops.

They turn on music they start to sing,
It really makes your ear drums ring,
They are greedy they are fat,
I hope they don't sit on my cat.

Rosie Moscrop (10)
Hambrook Primary School

BATTLESHIP

On the ship,
The mighty ship,
We defend tonight.

On the ship,
The mighty ship,
We attack tonight.

On the ship,
The mighty ship,
All the men will fight.

On the ship,
The mighty ship,
We want to win the fight.

On the ship,
The mighty ship,
We will win with might.

Jason Dayment (10)
Hambrook Primary School

I CAN'T DO IT!

How do I feel about a poem?
Even though I like them
I can't write them.
Come to think of it,
I've just done one!

Adam Slade (8)
Hambrook Primary School

MOON AND SUN

The sun shines bright up in the sky
Burning yellow, orange and red.
It gradually rises very high.
But hides away when we go to bed.

The sun shines on me and you.
While we laugh and play games.
It shines on everything we do.
But doesn't call us names.

The moon appears when it is dark.
And shines among the twinkling stars.
The earth below which it does light.
Only sees it every night.

The man in the moon watches over us all
As we sleep at night.
He is very quiet and lets us sleep
And he doesn't give us a fright.
He always has his midnight snack at night.

Hollie Godrich (10)
Hambrook Primary School

WINTER

The wind is blowing
And sometimes it's snowing,
The snow is falling,
The weather is appalling,
The cold weather is fun
But not as good as the sun.

Sophie Coleman (9)
Hambrook Primary School

SEASONS

Spring, spring
It will always win.
Pretty blossom is everywhere,
And sweet smells fill the air.

Summer, summer
It makes you happier.
It's nice to see the sun out smiling
Instead of people going on and whining.

Autumn, autumn,
The bare season.
Where different coloured leaves
Fall from their trees.

Winter, winter
Always a winner
Because nobody knows
Whether it will snow.

Seasons are the best!

Lydia Clayphan Turner (9)
Hambrook Primary School

FROG-SPAWN

There's a thousand bubbles
In our garden pool.
So slimy and like jelly
By the water it's made cool.

The fish gather round
At the amazing sight,
As the bubbles grow dots
The frogs grow life.

Emma Lerway (9)
Hambrook Primary School

HAPPINESS IN SEASONS

Summer, winter, autumn, spring,
They are the seasons that the world brings.
Summer is sunny and hot
While winter makes me cold a lot.
Autumn is when the leaves come down
Different colours red, yellow, brown.
Spring has to be the best
When birds sing without a rest.
I like having seasons all year round.
They make me happy when I am down.

Louise Harmer (10)
Hambrook Primary School

BIRDS

Birds, birds don't you know
Birds, birds how do you know
Birds, birds see them fly
Birds, birds come and fly
Birds, birds come for a bite
Birds, birds go and hide
Birds, birds come for a run
Birds, birds go for a run.

Richard Clay (10)
Hambrook Primary School

SPORTS DAY

Oh no it's sports day next day,
I don't know why it is in the middle of May.

That's the boy that wins the egg and spoon,
I think he is quite a loon.

There's the girl that wins the medal for hockey,
She's the one that's very cocky.

He's the one that is quite a cheat,
He has rather smelly feet.

My little brother, wants to bet,
On the day it's going to be wet.

I hope, I hope, I hope it's not,
If it is I'll tie his neck in a knot.

Ben Glastonbury (10)
Hambrook Primary School

POEM ABOUT FOOD

I would prefer fried eggs and ham,
To a tin of Tesco's spam.
I can't decide if I like shandy,
Better than a bottle of brandy.

I like foods that are hot and spicy,
But ice-cream can taste a tad bit icy.
I also like some Chinese food,
Italian meals are best if you're in a happy mood!

Frank Jayne (10)
Hambrook Primary School

FLOWERS

They glisten in the shining sun,
Wonderful and bright,
They're like a string of pretty pearls,
Beautiful and light.

Lovely petals multi-coloured,
Colourful and presently out of sight,
They hide away for the winter months,
Waiting for the new season of light.

They keep a watchful eye,
Over the children with their kite.
They could get it stuck in the tree,
You never know they just might.

Eliza George (11)
Hambrook Primary School

TENNIS

When I walked out on to the tennis court,
I saw this player who was very short.
He started to serve, he put on some swerve.
The ball came to me as fast as a bee
I whacked it back and it hit his knee.
Then I served a magic ace
To win the match, another trophy for the case.
'All in a day's work,' I said,
I shook hands with a player called Fred.
I lifted up the silver cup,
Next time it would bring me lots of luck.

Joshua Beale (11)
Hambrook Primary School

FIRST DAY AT SCHOOL

My first day at Steadfield School.
I was feeling very nervous.
I took a deep breath and left the car,
I felt like a total fool.

Reading was all right for some,
Everything was nice and quiet.
Then I saw the class teacher
This wasn't going to be fun.

When maths came it was not fine,
Talking drowned out everything.
I could not hear myself think,
Then finally came - playtime.

At playtime I found a friend called Lee,
He seemed to be quite nice.
Soon we had to line up,
Next lesson was RE.

RE was just as bad,
Somebody stepped out of line.
They were sent straight to class 1,
I would have to be a good lad.

Lunch-time did come and go,
I wanted to go home.
I could not stand another lesson,
My life had reached an all time low.

At home-time we came out late,
I wanted to go to bed.
When mum asked how school had been
I answered, 'It was great!'

Michael Crotch-Harvey (10)
Hambrook Primary School

PUPPIES

Puppies are sweet,
They're a real big treat.
They like to play,
And have their say.
Puppies play and run,
To have some fun.
They like to go on a walk,
I wish puppies could talk.

Puppies go out,
Without a doubt,
Especially when it shines,
They go out all the time.
Puppies give you their paw,
But not when it's sore.
They always go in the park,
To have a jolly good bark.

Charlotte Wall (10)
Hambrook Primary School

TEACHERS

Teachers, teachers in school.
They're big and long,
Their face like a bomb.
They're strict and mad,
They make fun of your dad,
Sometimes nice, sometimes bad.
They have smoke coming
Out of their ears and also
Some sweat coming out of their
Nose, but that's what teachers are like.

Lucy Harvey (8)
Headley Park Primary School

SMOOTH TREE

I saw a tree sparkle,
The leaves moved gently.

The branches rustled,
In the wind.

The tree grew bigger,
Like a child,
The roots got more wide.

But the best bit is,
It all looked back at me.

Amy Barnes (8)
Headley Park Primary School

MY MAGIC NANNY

My Nan is magic!

Her magic takes her everywhere,
She does not go by car,
And sometimes she takes you
Back in time.
One day,
It went wrong,
And she turned herself
Into a frog!

Gribbet!
Gribbet!

Charlotte Harris (8)
Headley Park Primary School

THE TITANIC

The Titanic sinking slowly,
How scary it must have been.
People dying for their family,
Crying sadly,
'Please don't die.'
People dying, people surviving.

When the Titanic filled up the water with its lights,
Then fading slowly, the water went dark.

But now we're still crying,
Because their families are dead.

Katie Daly (8)
Headley Park Primary School

STAR

Great star up in the sky,
      When you go past at night,
We can see it glowing in the sky,
      What a pretty sight.

Melissa Cockle (8)
Headley Park Primary School

JOEL

There was a boy called Joel,
Who didn't have a soul,
He kicked and he punched
All the children in a bunch
But then he got hit by a pole.

Bradley Roy Clark (10)
Henbury Court Junior School

MAGNOLIA TREE

I am a magnolia tree
My buds are pink and white
The colour of my trunk is green, grey, a bit of brown
I am lonely I hear noises all the time
I am getting old
My age is forty five
I am really old now
It is summer now
All my buds are out
My twigs are snapping
Children running around making noises
All around me are daffodils
Squirrels are climbing up me
Birds are sitting on me
I hear noises like sirens, bells, a machine and happy children
It's getting dark now
It is time for me to go to sleep now.

Kayleigh Hayward (9)
Henbury Court Junior School

TERRIFIED

Don't move.
It's only a spring.
No it's a long fish.
Its eyes are like marbles.
Its nasty grin its sharp.
It's on the move, it's going to bite me.
Tongue is sharp as an arrow.
It's bit me
I'm dying.

Christopher Parton (11)
Henbury Court Junior School

ALONE IN A FIELD

Alone in a field
So tall and so proud
Swaying with the wind
With only the rustling of my leaves
During the autumn they fall
I look very bare
But then in spring
My leaves grow again
Birds nesting
And children trying to climb my trunk
I've been here a long time
Alone in a field.

Kirsty Goodman (9)
Henbury Court Junior School

THE MAGNOLIA TREE

Under the small Magnolia tree
Lots of little bugs and things.
Lovely blossom in the summer and spring.
Children on the field playing sweetly.
Police cars, ambulances and fire engines
Sounds in the distance.
Little squirrels collecting nuts
Magpies on fences
At night time all is quiet -
Except foxes and things.

Adam Cavill (9)
Henbury Court Junior School

I LOVE FRECKLES

I Love freckles
Freckles is his name
Because he is dapple grey
He is thirteen hands high
He loves to eat apples and hay
I brush him every day
So he looks handsome
We love to run in the woods
We jump over things
You can guess who I love
Yes you know it's my horse.

Natasha Smith (8)
Henbury Court Junior School

SEASONS

Spring, summer, autumn, winter
Every year the same
Round and round the seasons go
Like a party game
Spin the leaves from green to gold
Turn the weather
Hot and cold
Chase the clouds across the sky
Paint a yellow sun
Then the rain comes
Tumbling down
Spoiling all our fun.

Sara Teymoor (9)
Henbury Court Junior School

THE GHOST STORY

The ghost that haunts our spooky house,
Is afraid of a tiny little mouse,
Every time it sees our den,
It clucks like a crazy hen,
One time when it saw our dog,
It hopped like a little frog,
The ghost that thinks he's so cool,
Has never been to Haunting School.

Rose Williams (9)
Henbury Court Junior School

MY GERBIL

My gerbil can run on the floor!
My fish can't!
My gerbil can jump!
My tamagotchi can't!
My gerbil can chew up loo rolls!
I can't!
My gerbil has got a long tail!
My fish hasn't!
My gerbil has got brown hair!
My tamagotchi hasn't!
My gerbil lives in a cage!
I can't - or can I?
And, no I'm not trying!

Andrew Thompson (10)
Henleaze Junior School

MIZEN'S HORIZON

This picture I like,
Looks like two mountains
With a lemon on the top
Of one mountain.
It makes you come,
It makes you stop
Mountains are very beautiful.

Jennifer Sarah Mu (8)
Henleaze Junior School

I ONCE SAW THIS PICTURE

I once saw this picture by
                    Laura Thomas
It was calm and gentle
With a rocket ready to blast off
                    It is style!
It makes me want to be in her
                    Picture.

Katie Fuller (9)
Henleaze Junior School

WINTER IS HERE

Winter is here,
And spring is near,
But summer is done,
Just like the sun.

Lucy Harrison (10)
Henleaze Junior School

WORK

Ding-a-ling-ding
With a ding-a-long-dong,
All my work's gone wrong, wrong, wrong.

It's filled up the trash cans,
And every single bin
Each and every one of them
Up to the rim.

All my work is awful writing,
It looks like it's been struck by lightning.

Ding-a-ling-ding
With a ding-a-long-dong,
All my work's gone wrong, wrong, wrong.

Patrick Duffy (11)
Henleaze Junior School

FISH

I saw a fish
Swimming in the sea
I saw a fish
Looking at me.

The fish was swimming
As fast as a Cheetah
Along came another
I thought it would beat her.

The fish were racing
Right under my feet
The one I saw first
I thought it would cheat.

Clare Hollinghurst (9)
Henleaze Junior School

KING HENRY VIII

King Henry VIII
Was a happy chap
He loved to sing
And dance and chat
He ate a lot and grew so fat
He never knew how fat he was!

Kayleigh Hackett (9) & Laura Thomas (8)
Henleaze Junior School

WE LIKE SPEAKING NONSENSE

N obody knows what I did tomorrow,
O ld people come with sorrow.
N obody knows what I did the day after tomorrow.
S tupid sentences they seem to be,
E nd this fight with me and Lee,
N onsense we seem to speak,
S ends us off . . . off to sleep,
E ating ice-cream in the park, end this poem
                            before it gets dark.

Sarah Bird & Ava Palfrey (10)
Henleaze Junior School

THE RABBIT

The rabbit is a furry creature,
It has some really cute features.
The rabbit hops about all day,
He likes to sleep in the hay.
For me rabbits are number one,
They are the best and really fun.

Simon Day (10)
Henleaze Junior School

THE FUNFAIR

The funfair starts at eleven o'clock,
The lights come on the music plays!
The gates are open the crowds come in.
The Ghost House is scary, yells and screams come out of it,
And people come out white in the face!
The roller-coaster is really fun but does make you feel sick,
The Big Wheel is very high up and make sure you don't look down!

Tom Biddulph (11)
Henleaze Junior School

FOR AN ELEPHANT

Big,
Grey,
Animal.

Tom Foster (10)
Henleaze Junior School

MY FRIEND IS ALWAYS THERE

My friend is always there for me,
Like if we want to play a game,
Or if we want to do something the same,
He will lend me a hand,
Like if I need help in a band,
And I know he'll always be there,
And that's the same with me.

Sean Barrett (10)
Henleaze Junior School

GHOSTS

They come out at the dead of night
They give my friends a terrible fright
They scare them all half to death
They also have stinky breath
But I think ghosts are wonderful and weird
They probably hide in my uncle's beard
They make weird sounds like *boo* or *ooo*
Do not worry they're just trying to scare you.

Alison Tyrrell (10)
Henleaze Junior School

THE MONSTER

In the middle of the night the monster lurked.
Looking for people to crunch and slurp.
But dear Prince Charming hit the monster with a whack
So the monster chopped off his head with a great big smack.
The prince was dead.
The monster ate his head.
And the next night.
He came back.

Kayleigh Godfrey (10)
Henleaze Junior School

TEA

I can't wait for my tea,
My tummy's all rumbling inside of me,
I've, carrots, peas and chips for tea,
Hurry up mum or I'll be
Really, really hungry.

Jenny Read (10)
Henleaze Junior School

THE GREEN MAN PROTECTING HIS TREE

There stands a big oak in a field,
Where the Green Man once was killed.
He was protecting his tree,
When came over little young Lee.
The Green Man jumped down,
But broke his crown,
Then little, young Lee
Jumped to his knees and stabbed him in the back.
The Green Man gave a scream and then fell to his dream.

Holly Daniel (11)
Henleaze Junior School

IMAGINATION

If you look underwater,
And you're in the right place,
I can guarantee that you will see,
A fish with a brace.

Yes a fish with a brace,
If you're in the right place,
Is a common thing to see,
As well as coral playing chase.

If you're wondering what I'm on about,
You'll soon know if you read on,
Everybody has it,
It's called your *im-ag-in-a-tion!*

Katherine Hooper (10)
Henleaze Junior School

THE CHIMPANZEE

Chips are clever,
Chimps are smart,
Chimps can also make you laugh,
But still they're very dangerous,
If you give a little stare,
He will attack,
And you might get a hefty whack.

Stephen Bond (11)
Henleaze Junior School

THE DIAMANTÉ POEM

Man
Thin, tall
Eating, looking punching
Skin, hair   sea, cold
Singing, swimming, Jumping,
Long, beautiful
dolphin.

Janec Lillis-James (10)
Henleaze Junior School

ALIENS!

What are aliens? People say
They come from planets far away.
But what on earth will scientists do?
When we start saying, we're aliens too!
Perhaps they'll argue but guess what?
They'll probably argue quite a lot!

Keith Croft (10)
Henleaze Junior School

MY MONSTER

I have a little monster,
It lives under my bed.
I can't look under it,
Or it might grab my head.

When I clean my teeth,
I crouch down very low.
So when I go past my bed,
It won't catch my toe.

When I am in bed,
I tuck myself right in.
And sometimes I think it's crawling,
Right inside my bin.

I have a little monster,
It lives under my bed.
I can't look under it,
Or it might grab my head.

Cecily Moore (10)
Henleaze Junior School

WOMBLES

I think wombles are really cool,
They're just like a really fluffy ball.
They have got a song I can't get out of my head,
I even sing it when I'm in bed.

Wombles are the only thing on my mind,
Because there's nothing else I can find.
They live in something called a burrow,
Which they clean out very thorough.

Chloe Manning (10)
Henleaze Junior School

MR MONKEY GEORGE

Mr Monkey George
Happy as can be
But he's in a cage
Sitting next to me.

George's best friend,
Called Mrs Molly Gee,
She's his monkey friend
And she's climbing up a tree.

So you see Monkey George,
Is quite happy really,
But he's in a cage
Sitting next to me.

Portia Abraham (10)
Henleaze Junior School

THE CROCODILE

The crocodile has rough, scaly skin,
And rusty, dusty coloured legs.
With a pointed snout and fine teeth
And a tail that swishes and wallops around.

A rough back and small legs,
And bulging, mean eyes.
It swims around and looks at you,
And tries to catch its meal.

Amy Travers (10)
Henleaze Junior School

A LONELY FISH

A lonely fish in the sea,

L ots of things used to fill him with glee.
O ctopuses, crabs and eels,
N ought per-cent survived the rod and reels.
E verybody laughed at him 'cause
L onely fish speaks in a buzz
Y onks and yonks passed like this,

F or lonely fish sounds like a fizz
I n the end of course he died,
S harks and whales ate his side.
H orrid life had lonely fish.

Eddie Notton (10)
Henleaze Junior School

RABBIT'S JOURNEY

Running on, on and on
    Must get there, must get there
        Will I make it, will I make it?
            Racing on, on and on
                Foraging here, foraging there
                    Must get food, must get food
                        Not very much, not very much
                            I will live, I will live
                                Nearly there, nearly there
                                    Here we are, here we are
                                        The long journey's end.

Lydia Brown (9)
Henleaze Junior School

THE DUST MITE

The dust mite, the dust mite,
He must bite.
When the vacuum comes along
He'll get sucked up,
Bite a hole in the bag,
Stick 'is head out, sing a song.
The dust mite, the dust mite,
He must bite.

George Evans (10)
Henleaze Junior School

ANIMALS

Soft, furry, fluffy, fun, rabbit.
Slimy, slithery, smooth snake,
It doesn't matter what they're like,
They're just made perfectly right.

Emily Browne (10)
Henleaze Junior School

BETHLEHEM

O little town of Bethlehem,
I see that baby weep,
All wrapped up in rags,
In a dreamless sleep.

Michael Lewis (10)
Henleaze Junior School

THERE ONCE WAS A DRAGON

There once was a dragon named Dave
He lived in a beautiful cave.

There once was a dragon named Fred.
He had a little white bed.

There once was a dragon named Bert,
He always played in the dirt.

There once was a dragon named Sean,
For dinner he ate frog-spawn.

There once was a dragon named Joe
His wings were as white as snow.

Colleen Barrett (7)
Henleaze Junior School

TIGER

Tiger's eyes shining bright,
Glowing yellow in the night.
When I caught it in my sight,
It gave me an almighty fright.
I thought her coat had caught on fire,
Though I couldn't help admire,
The jet-black stripes that lay upon,
Her coat that went along,
Its graceful body great and strong

Chelsea Hackett (11)
Henleaze Junior School

A LAMENT FROM CABOT'S WORST ENEMY

Oh! I hate being on the Matthew,
Doing all the work,
I wish it would be over, phew!
And, I can't even iron my shirt.

Being on the Matthew,
Is worse than being in jail,
In jail they're having all the fun,
While I'm working on the sail.

The King's shilling that I have,
I can't even spend,
But still, it is quite useful,
At home, I'd spend it before the weekend.

Olivia Heenan (10)
Henleaze Junior School

SOPHIE'S LIFE

I'm Sophie.
I'm 6.
My bed's blue.
My teddy's pink.
I need a drink.
But not always.
I'm glad I'm 6.
But it's nicer to be 7.
I like life.
So does my mum.

Timothy Stephen Merchant (11)
Henleaze Junior School

CHRISTMAS

I am excited because it's Christmas Eve
And I am at my cousin's house.
We are telling each other funny jokes
And drinking coke.
My brother held a raffle
And I won a Galaxy chocolate bar.
My aunt made a cake
And laid it on the table.
I was first to get a piece
We went back home
And went to watch the Harry Enfield Special
I woke up from bed
After what seemed like a minute.
But it was Christmas Day!

David Wilkinson (8)
Henleaze Junior School

THE BEANO BOOK

The Beano Book is very funny.
Even though you want the money.
Gnasher and Dennis,
Are such a menace.
Even a man is funny in the Beano Book.
It's like a real thing happening.
It's the best comic book
      Ever.

Craig Helps (10)
Henleaze Junior School

WHY DID IT HAVE TO BE ME?

Why did it have to be me?
My wife doesn't even know,
I hate boats, I hate heights
And sailing's not my cup of tea.

John Cabot says that if we don't
Do all the work he says,
He'll get us alone to scrub the decks,
Or he'll push us overboard
And he always get me to climb the riggings,
Knowing full-well I hate heights.

The biscuits are revolting, there's maggots all over 'em,
My cabin mate has scurvy,
A rotten disease that he's caught,
And when I counted the scars on his face there were 110.

Why did it have to be me,
There could be a monster out there,
I'm scared of heights, I'm seasick,
Oh why did it have to be me?

Miriam Myerscough (10)
Henleaze Junior School

THE TIGER

The tiger prowls behind a tree,
He does not want to be seen you see.
Don't worry the tiger is not shy,
But tonight he'd like buffalo pie.

Soon the tiger will be hungry again,
His hunger will be horrible,
His tummy will rumble,
His stomach will tumble,
So be careful when the tiger is hungry again.

Ellen Hardiman (9)
Henleaze Junior School

THAT DREADED DAY

I woke up early in the morning,
Just as the day was dawning,
Mum got me up and started getting me ready,
I grumbled, 'What's the rush? Steady, steady!'
She answered, 'On the train you shall ride,
You're going to the countryside.'
We got to the station, she let go of my wrist,
And then upon my cheek she kissed.
She said goodbye, and then she cried, 'I love you,
Have a good ride.'
I shed a tear upon the train,
For my heart was full of pain.
When I got to the hall,
I was picked by Mrs Paul.
I had a good time, I made a friend,
I read the letters that my mum did send.
I thought of my mum every day,
While I would help Mrs Paul stack the hay,
And after a bit, I got used to it,
For if I had stayed in the city
Who knows where I would be.

Thomas Polyviou (11)
Henleaze Junior School

WHEN I WAS HAPPY

I felt very amazed
When it was my 6th birthday.
Because I had an amazing surprise.
I could tell there was something going on.
By the exciting look on their faces.
I went to Disneyland.
I was totally thrilled.
My brother was also excited.
I was really happy.
I had gone red in the face.
It took about eighteen hours to get there
Because of a big traffic jam.
My brother and I got really bored
Just looking at grass and black and brown cows.

David Cook (8)
Henleaze Junior School

A SAILOR'S MOAN

Being hit round the head from our jails
To a massive boat with sails.
Eating rotten food from the barrels,
I try to cheer myself up with carols.
Changing the sails and scrubbing the deck,
Really gives me a pain in the neck.
With the crashing of waves it fills me with fright,
Sometimes I wonder if I'll live through the night.
I don't know where we're going it could be to Rome,
I just would to know when we're going home.

James Richards (11)
Henleaze Junior School

AT THE CIRCUS

Once I was so amazed
When I went to the circus.
I was amazed because
I saw men eating fire.
The flame looked orange
And yellow.
In my head I was thinking about
My fire at home.
How it crackled.
How it was so warm.
We watched lots of other amazing things.
We had some candyfloss
And then we went home.

Hilary Orchard (8)
Henleaze Junior School

WHEN I WAS EXCITED

One day I was at school.
And I knew my mum was in hospital.
Then when my dad and gran came.
They told me that my mum had a baby boy.
At five o'clock we took some food and a present
And when I saw him,
I was thinking inside me
I wish I could hold him.
I smelled something horrible,
The coffee!

Panna Jethwa (7)
Henleaze Junior School

ASHAMED OF WHAT I HAVE DONE

I felt bad
My mum asked me to do something
And I did not do it.
I felt ashamed
Of what I did to my mum.
I went to do what she asked me to do,
But it was done.
So I said I was sorry
And hugged mummy.

Katy Dee (8)
Henleaze Junior School

BEING FRIENDS

In the morning,
There wasn't a cloud in the sky.
I played cricket
With my friends.
I was happy.

Johnathan Hyde (7)
Henleaze Junior School

THE FISH THAT SWAM

If a fish lived down my street
When he went to town I'd drown
And if he saw a killer whale
I'd be in bed growing a tale.

Duncan Bambridge (10)
Henleaze Junior School

FRIEND

I have a friend, she's very loyal.
We're mad at times with Sarah Doyle.
I know I can trust this person with all my heart.
She's the greatest friend and in most things she will take part.
She's smart, clever and just a bit mad.
Never ever mean or sad.
She is great at writing and talking too.
She will always have time to play with you.
Her clothes are cool, funky and new.
She sometimes scares you too!
My brilliant, caring, thoughtful friend.
I will like her until the end.
The person I am writing about
Is Katrina Hornsey without a doubt.

Josephine Hall (11)
Henleaze Junior School

THE GOLDEN EAGLE

I looked at it amazed
I looked at its golden feathers
I couldn't believe I was looking at it.
I studied its long slender body
Suddenly it spread its magnificent wings and flew off.
Suddenly my mum took a picture of it.
A picture of a Golden Eagle.

Matthew McCoubrey (7)
Henleaze Junior School

A FRIEND INDEED

My best friend has a wonderful smile,
If you measured it, it would last a mile.
She is pretty, happy, funky and loyal,
Her heart could make Jack Frost, himself boil.

All her happiness and care,
When I'm sad she'll always share.
If we were chained together, it wouldn't worry me,
Because she'll always keep me happy, and busy as a bee.

When I'm hungry and have nothing to eat,
She'll always offer me something sweet.
To me she is all that a friend should be,
And what makes it special, she's a friend to me.

Susannah Hopkins (10)
Henleaze Junior School

A GOOD FRIEND

A good friend is someone who is loyal,
They don't have to be royal.
They don't need to have much cash,
Or a swimming pool to splash.
They don't have to be as strong as a tiger,
They don't have to be as small as a badger.
It doesn't matter if their parents are senile,
Or they are vile.
A friend has to be sharing and caring.
A good friend is all of that,
One of mine is called Matt.

Hugo Gemal (10)
Henleaze Junior School

A FRIEND FOR ME

A friend for me
Would have to be
Not superduper, wonderful and flash
Or loaded up with heaps of cash
A good friend for me
Would have to be
Generous and kind, so when you fall
They help you stand up straight and tall
A good friend for me
Doesn't have to be
Great at English or wonderful at art
Or totally brainy and amazingly smart
That's what a good friend for me
Would have to be
A friend like that would be fine
And that sounds like some of the friends of mine.

Sarah Doyle (11)
Henleaze Junior School

MY BEST FRIEND

Funny, cool, hates school.
He's in my class, loves pool.
But he's never cruel.

Clever, smart, always does a fart.
Likes computers, likes pea shooters.
Loves girls, has no curls.

Helpful, kind, not tall, but I don't mind.
Always helpful, never doubtful.
But most of all, he's the best friend I've ever had.

Alex Thoemmes (11)
Henleaze Junior School

A BEST FRIEND

I felt upset,
Lonely,
Unwanted,
All I needed
Was a bit of help.

A bit of sharing,
Kindness,
Loyalty,
All I wanted
Was a bit of help.

Then all that came,
Wittily,
Wisely,
In the form
Of my best friend Jo.

All that happiness,
Warmth,
Friendship,
That's why I like
My best friend Jo.

Hannah Greenslade (10)
Henleaze Junior School

FRIENDSHIP

A good friend to me
Is someone like Leanne
She's not like Doyle
But of course Doyle is loyal.

Leanne is not royal
And not full of oil
She smells like a rose
Doesn't pick her nose
Also doesn't pose.

Caroline Davies (10)
Henleaze Junior School

MY FRIEND

My friend never stands any nonsense at all
and always puts me right.
She cheers me up when I am down
and can't stand a fight.

She mostly feels like my sister
when she gives me love and care.
She's as sparkly as the sun
and her personality is rare.

We used to live on Newton Road
round the corner was our school.
We used to go to the cinema
and the swimming pool.

I've known her since I was in my cot
and guzzling baby food.
Our friendship is like a spiral
it will never end for good.

The miles don't matter
even though she's far away.
Until we meet again
I'll think about her every day.

Sarah Rudston (10)
Henleaze Junior School

THE LION

The lion leaps
With all its might.
Watch out! Be careful!
It will give you a fright
And if you can run
He'll give chase.
Be careful of his
Giant pace,
And if you get eaten
Bit by bit
He'll spit your bones out,
Spit, spit, spit.

Henry Reed (9)
Henleaze Junior School

THE FRENCH ROAST

The French eat most peculiar things
for their Sunday roast.
Like beetle bums smothered in rum
and snail and lettuce toast.
Now take a zombie's liver
and boil it in a stew.
Then add a lizard's tail
scales and spikes complete.
So there's a little taster
of what they like to eat.

William Banfield (10)
Henleaze Junior School

A GOOD FRIEND

A good friend is kind and makes you
feel great to be with them.
Like a warm feeling inside.
My special friend is Amy.
It's hard for me to write this poem,
because there's so many ways of
describing her.
Well here's a few.
Funny.
Who will put a tickle inside your belly.
A good friendship
like a circle that never ends.
It's like a good book that you can't put down.
Kind.
She's kind and caring and acts like a dog,
but never a frog.
Clever.
She's clever and will never boast.
I like her the most!

Sarah Young (11)
Henleaze Junior School

TITANIC

It was a most upsetting night that gave us all quite a fright.
Water rushing, bursting in.
People screaming, yelling and shouting.
People wondering where the next lifeboat was going to be
and how to stop the children crying.
Finally the ship went down and, oh good gracious, what a sound!
People yelling and screaming in agony and finally they all passed out.

Jonathan Cross (9)
Henleaze Junior School

TITANIC!

Titanic was called the ship of dreams,
With all its shine and shimmering gleam.
People came from far and near,
To see this piece of laughter and cheer.
Unsinkable they said it was,
Before it scraped that icy rock.
People drowned because of them,
Not enough lifeboats for the men.
Two thousand two hundred and a whole twenty eight,
Were on that ship when it came to its fate.
A mere few hundred were saved from the wreck,
While most of the rest died on the deck.
So that's the story of the masterful ship,
That sunk on its awful maiden trip.

Anna Thorp (10)
Henleaze Junior School

THE LEPRECHAUN

Faster than light,
he is such a sight,
the leprechaun on the green,
it's a pity that he, the leprechaun,
has never been actually seen!

Jumping, leaping,
slowly creeping,
the leprechaun on the green,
it's a pity that he, the leprechaun,
has never been actually seen!

Selene Nelson (9)
Henleaze Junior School

THE BULLY AND THE FRIEND

There once came a day
When I went out to play
There was a huge boy
Who said to me 'Oi!'
He said 'Come over here'
And he pinched my ear
Now my friend Philip Wren
Came up to me then
He told me 'Come on'
As if nothing was wrong!
So we both walked away
And I shouted 'Hooray!'
The bully just stared
I knew my friend really cared.

Alex Corcoran (10)
Henleaze Junior School

DISNEY WORLD

I felt excited when I read my invitation
                    to Disney World Paris.
Stephen and I were jumping
all over the sofa.
Guess you've figured
we were excited eh?
We still can't wait to go.
It seems a shame
it's in March.

David Cutler (8)
Henleaze Junior School

FRIENDS

I have a very special friend,
Our friendship will never end,
The good friend I am referring to,
Is Katriana who's brainy too.

Another good friend of mine,
Is Jo who's good and kind,
She is cool and still at school,
But I don't really mind.

The last friend of mine,
Is Lauren who is really kind,
She doesn't mind if you're unkind,
But these are the friends of mine.

Wallis Jozefowicz (10)
Henleaze Junior School

A RABBIT'S POINT OF VIEW

When I get up in the morning,
Just as Robert's yawning,
In my mind I have no doubt,
When he comes down he'll clean me out.

He'll take my bowl and give me a feed,
When I'm in a time of need,
When Kizzy decides to sprout,
Then you see my nose pop out.

When I eat Rob's mum's sage,
Rob comes up and puts me back in my cage.

Robert Weaver (10)
Henleaze Junior School

MY FRIEND BEN

I once had a friend called Ben Jones,
And it wasn't that far back I s'pose,
But then one day my mother chose,
To tell me he'd moved to Amberland's Close,
I was very upset about Ben,
Because he'd been my best friend till then,
But as luck would have it,
The very next day,
Alex Thoemmes arrived,
Hip, hip, hooray,
And when he saw me,
I wondered if we,
Could get on well,
And lucky for me,
The following day,
Alex Thoemmes came round to play,
And as I look back on when I was 9,
I'm just glad Alex Thoemmes got here in time.

Nick Lismore-John (11)
Henleaze Junior School

FRIENDS

I have a few special friends,
Our loyalty never ends.
A friend of mine does not have to be
As clever as can be.
My friends have helped me through thick and thin
And all the happiness comes from within.
So go on find your friend today
And in your life you'll find little sun rays.

Louise Hammonds (11)
Henleaze Junior School

JOSEPH IS A FRIEND OF MINE

Joseph is a friend of mine, he's very loyal to me.
He comes to me whether I'm sad or happy.
He plays with me all day.
He sticks with me from thin to thick and
Everything I go through.
Joseph is a very good friend, I couldn't wish for more.

Aron Szekely (10)
Henleaze Junior School

THE PARK

Down at the park
where the trains go by
and there are cricket matches going on
we go and play on the swings and slides
until it's
time to go home . . .

Abigail Corcoran (8)
Henleaze Junior School

CATS

Cats sleep anywhere, any window, any chair.
Any place anywhere, cats sleep anywhere.
Cats doze in the sun.
They play and have fun.
Chasing mice until the day is done.
My cat always sits next to the fire,
While I'm doing my homework, it's rather a tire.

Matthew Watts (10)
Henleaze Junior School

MY FRIENDS

They don't have to be tall,
But they have to be cool,
This funky friend is Josephine Hall.

If she was to go
She would be greatly missed,
Of her good qualities I could make a list,
This special friend is Alison Grist.

She is a very good friend of mine,
She is always there, and for you she has time,
This caring friend is Caroline.

This person is good to me
She is weird (funnily).
This wacky friend is loyal Lea.

Katrina Hornsey (11)
Henleaze Junior School

A POEM FOR MY FRIEND

I have a very special friend,
And I hope that our friendship will never end,
A friend does not have to be,
Big, small or wear glasses like me.

If I hurt or cut my knee,
She comes and takes care of me,
The friend that I have in mind,
Is Katrina who's good and kind.

Alison Grist (10)
Henleaze Junior School

THERE WAS A YOUNG MAN

There was a young man from Bombay,
Who slid down the stairs on a tray,
Bumped into the Queen, said 'Sorry old bean
But you shouldn't of got in the way.'

Byron Stadden (10)
Henleaze Junior School

FLOWERS

Flowers, flowers,
how do they grow?
From a seed I guess, but do I really know?
They survive in the winter.
They survive in the snow.
Flowers, flowers how do they grow?

Kirstie Hillman (9)
Henleaze Junior School

FRUIT

Fruit is juicy,
It tastes so mouth-watering,
Once you take a bite you go pale white,
Then you go bright green like a kiwi,
Then you go back to your normal colour,
But when you try a lemon,
It tastes so sour it's got loads of power,
So basically I'm saying that fruit
Is lovely, but don't try a lemon, trust me.

Faye Harvey (10)
Henleaze Junior School

THE RUSHING RIVER

The rushing river calm and still
flowing along the rocky hill, but
suddenly the river changes over and
under, hitting and spitting, rushing
down through the valley, and it slows
to enter the sea and that's the
last of the river you will ever see.

Jordan Paul (9)
Henleaze Junior School

THE STAINED GLASS WINDOW

The stained glass window,
was a glass picture of a lake.
It was blue,
with a few other colours.
It was double glazed
and UPVC.
That was the stained glass window.

Jonathan Morgan (10)
Henleaze Junior School

THE SOLAR SYSTEM

Neptune is blue
And Saturn is brown
But the sun is orange
Why are planets and stars different colours?
Why?
  Why?
    Why?

Edmund Hinton (9)
Henleaze Junior School

TEACHERS!

My teacher Mrs Spot,
She loves a lot of things,
She goes around accusing you,
Of things you didn't do,
But have you seen her shopping,
Chickens, turkeys and muffins,
I must admit she is quite fat,
Even though she likes it like that,
She lets us do fun things,
In school like playing pool.
Mrs Spot you're so cool!

Kayo Titiloye (9)
Henleaze Junior School

LAYLORD

Laylord has got a little tail.
I mean a little, little tail.
It is smaller than a cat's tail.
It is smaller than a dog's tail.
It is smaller than a lion's tail.
It is smaller than a cheetah's tail.
It is smaller than a chimpanzee's tail.
It is smaller than a tiger's tail.
It is smaller than a mouse's tail.
It is only 1cm long.

Carmelo Cocchiara (9)
Henleaze Junior School

A GOOD FRIEND POEM

I have a friend who's very kind
She has a very brainy mind
We like to talk and play
And she comes to my house to stay.

If I fall down
She makes me laugh by being a clown
I hope we'll be friends until I die
Only then will I say bye bye.

Laura Cass (11)
Henleaze Junior School

FRIENDS

Loyalty that's a friend,
Sticks with you till the end,
Never leaves you,
Always believes you,
That's what makes a friend.

A friend never lets you down,
Treats you like a royal crown,
Whether you're tall,
Or very small,
That's what makes a friend.

Stephanie Aldrich (10)
Henleaze Junior School

AUTUMN YEAR

When autumn creeps up you shiver.
Squirrels dashing in and out of their holes.
Running to get nuts.
Leaves all brown and crisp.
Badgers already asleep.
When it's cold, wind blows.
Leaves fall down to their death.
Raindrops dropping drip, drop, drip, drop!

Sasha Squires (9)
Henleaze Junior School

THE BEACH

When I go to the caravan,
I always go on the beach.
Sometimes I take my cousin and go
looking for crabs.
When we find a crab it always goes
'Nip! Nip!'
When we've finished, the tide comes
in s*plash!* and then the waves come in.
It grows big like a *monster* and makes
a loud *splash.*
After the tide goes out the floor is soggy,
slodge, squidge.
When we've finished at the beach
we walk home for tea, *crunch, crunch.*

Matthew Grant (9)
Holymead Junior School

SING BIRD

A bird sings tweet, tweet, tweet
My oh my in spring, spring, spring
Sitting on the wall little blue tit
Come and sing all day long
Little bluebird tweet, tweet, tweet
It's dinnertime my little bird
After dinner come and dance
When sunset falls
Night is here
The next morning
Sun is up and sing and dance all day long.

Rebecca Budd (9)
Holymead Junior School

FOREST

A twig in the forest, click! click! click!
The trees in your way, rattle! rattle! rattle!
Sticky leaves, sticky! sticky! sticky!
Animals licking the water fast, lick! lick! lick!
The sound of animals chasing each other
in the water, splash! splash! splash!
Trees shaped like a
Monster staring at you
You run home as scared as scared can be.

Rebecca Taylor (9)
Holymead Junior School

FIRE!

It moves round the house burning everything.
The smoke floats round the house and causes smog.
The fire goes *crackle! crackle!*
You wonder what to do.
You shut all the doors and call 999.
You ask for a fire engine, it comes right on time.
They put out the fire with their mighty hose.
Then you thank them very much.

Michal Eddolls (8)
Holymead Junior School

WOOF

He barks at me *arrr -*
Rof! rof! rof! he taps on
Windows, arrr! arrr! arrr!
He was looking at me
A big dog staring at me.

Scott Saunders (9)
Holymead Junior School

GOING FISHING

When I go fishing I never catch
a thing. My dad would catch
a pike and my sister will
catch an old bike, but I
never catch a thing.

Josh Short (9)
Holymead Junior School

SUPER HERO

Over the planets, the moon, the stars,
there is man on cold, cold Mars.
You would think he was frozen but
you're wrong, he's as warm as a light.
But you think 'What does he do?'
Well I'll tell you.
When there's a fight on planet Earth,
he will come and sort it out.
He's been like this since his birth.
He used to play with his evil brother, Meville.
His name sounds innocent but you're wrong.
He's been evil for so long.
You could see he was evil from his birth -
his eyebrows curled, his frown as big as a boomerang,
his mind so evil, his frown so hard.
Stuck a safety pin in his brother.
That's how she died -from shock, poor old mother.

Cate Totney (8)
Holymead Junior School

TIGERS

In the jungle, tigers *rrr!*
And eat other animals
Climb up trees all day long
Hunt at night
Sleep at daytime
Run round the jungle catching their prey
Eating it up a tree
Jumping into rivers *splash, splash!*
They go jumping into rivers.

Andrew Webber (8)
Holymead Junior School

SAFARI

The jeep I ride I look out of the window
and see elephants squirting water at themselves.
When they see us they run after us with their
trunks full of water. When we go into the forest
we see tigers fighting. Quickly step on it, here
they come. As we go zooming through the
forest we lose them. Then as quick as a flash
we're back home.

Nicholas Cockram (9)
Holymead Junior School

FISH

The cod and the trout
swim for their lives.
Up the streams and down the rivers.
They swim forever and a day.
Some fish don't make this journey.

Rachel Witcombe (9)
Holymead Junior School

SOUND

When I go to the swimming pool
All the splashing when people jump in
And all the water splashing up getting people wet
All the water going over the edge
All the splashing getting people wet.

Steven Adams (9)
Holymead Junior School

FORGOTTEN CHILDHOOD

She was sitting on a huge elm tree branch.
In her pale, skinny hands she was holding some rough rags.
She also had a rusty needle that she was pricking
her pale, skinny, bony hands with.
Her eyes were raining tears.
Suddenly she dropped everything on the swishing grass.
She dug her head into her pale, skinny, bony, milky hands and
sobbed her eyes out.
I knew I had seen her before.
She quickly looked up with a frightened look.
She fell off the branch and pricked her pale, skinny, bony,
milky, sore hands.

Jenny Edgecombe (9)
Holymead Junior School

THE BEACH

The waves go lap, lap,
Like the birds go flap, flap.
The adults go chat, chat,
The children go clap, clap.
At the end of the day
A great big
Hairy and fat
Monster
Comes out to play.
He has a very nice day.

Katie Williams (9)
Holymead Junior School

MONSTER

Monster Monster I hear a monster
I get out of bed,
I turn round the corner and,
What do I see, a great big monster
looking down at me.
It snarls, snarls like that at me.
I look behind and see a baby monster.
Then suddenly somebody shouts *surprise*
and what do I see,
it's only my friends just dressed up
in a monster suit.

Laura Hudd (8)
Holymead Junior School

PLANETS

Over the moon and far away
All of the planets come to say
'Please do not litter.'
One planet said 'I've got loads
and it really feels horrible.'
The Milky Way came woooooooshing beside
and said 'IIII haaavee nooot goooott liiiiitter.'
And Mercury said 'Oooky so gooo away.'
'Oooh poor Milky Way they always make fun of hhim.
Helpp whatt's haaapeening tooo meee
oooh noo III've goooot it nnnnnowww.'

Stacey Roberts (9)
Holymead Junior School

COSMIC

Cosmic the man, the strong man was whizzing
through the air trying to get to space, but he
wasn't there. Higher and higher, bigger and
bigger, closer and finally he had landed on the
moon, and sat on the top and had cherryade
his mother had just made for him, and then
Cosmic said bye. He started his engine then
woosh. He came zooming down, rushing.

Lisa Collier (9)
Holymead Junior School

RABBIT

Ears like carrots,
Tail like a fluffy ball,
Claws like pins,
Body like a giant fluffy egg,
Paws like hairy circles,
Dainty as a fairy,
Head as a lopsided ball.

Jennifer Skuse (8)
Holymead Junior School

MOTHERS ARE . . .

Caring and cuddly
Lovely and incredible
Beautiful and giggly
Thanking and caring
Forever kind.

Lucy Egan (9)
Holymead Junior School

THE BLOODY BATTLE OF WATERLOO

The swooshing of swords.
The shouting of generals.
The banging of a gun, a bullet flies through the air
and hits a man.
The crying of that man in pain and then all
goes quiet as he falls to the ground.
The battle is over, hear and see the mothers
and children crying,
as they squelch through the dead bodies.
Hear the trees whispering and whooshing in
the wind.
Just see dead bodies moaning over the battlefield
that does not stand today.

Emily Thompson (9)
Holymead Junior School

HAIKUS

Mist Haiku

Mist is secretive,
A silk cover for the sky,
Mist is white as milk.

Sea Haiku

The sea gleams brightly,
It can be extremely rough,
But it can calm down.

Richard Harley (9)
Holymead Junior School

IN THE SEA

In the sea it is dark.
There are fish swimming around
The dark and gloomy sea.
People throwing in their fishing rods.
People riding in their boats.
Going over the slushy seaweed.
You can see the dolphins leaping out from the sea.
Electric eels lighting up the dark sea.
People throwing stones in the sea.

David Swatton (8)
Holymead Junior School

MEMORIES

The great azure sky
reflecting on the sea.
The mountains are thick with snow
and as tall as can be.

These are my memories.

The blinding sun is shining.
The waves are crashing into rocks
and the wind whistles down the road.

These are my memories.

Alexandra Farley (9)
Holymead Junior School

THE JUNGLE

In the deep dark and dense jungle
It's never silent
Trees groan and creak
And on the leaves there is a tip tap of raindrops.

The heat scorches the animals
As they slowly trudge to the whooshing river
The animals slurp cool refreshing water
And on the leaves there is a tip tap of raindrops.

Roars can be heard from miles away
And the river gushes along
The honey bees hum merrily
And on the leaves there is a tip tap of raindrops.

Squawking fills the land
With cheeps everywhere
Quacks also join in
And on the leaves there is a tip tap of raindrops.

And the wind howls along
The trees being to whisper
The wind rustles and crunches leaves
And on the leaves there is a tip tap of raindrops.

Samantha Orchard (9)
Holymead Junior School

WINTER

On a cold winter's day
The snow is falling
The sky is grey and misty
And the lakes are all frozen up.

An old man is coming down the road
He is very upset
He sees the street all grey and misty
So he runs home.

Stacey Davies (8)
Holymead Junior School

MY DOG IS . . .

My dog is black as ebony
Her paws are pink as a face
Her ears are floppy like a rabbit
She is cute and cuddly
But she's got some bad habits.

Josie Keegan (9)
Holymead Junior School

DOWN MY STREET

The leaves swoosh down the pavement
And the trees sway to and fro in the sky
Rain drips off the flowers
The wind blows in my hair
But soon dawn will come
So I can go to sleep in my bed
And get ready for a new fresh day.

Zoe Chapman (9)
Holymead Junior School

MOTHERS ARE . . .

Young or old
Cute and rude
Beautiful but bizarre
Super but smelly
Giggly but old fashioned
Kind but gets on my nerves
Incredible softies
So that's the embarrassing *mums!*

Alex Cook (9)
Holymead Junior School

BEAUTIFUL FIREWORKS

I like pretty fireworks
They look like stars in the sky
It's spread across the sky quickly
I'm excited
I like watching fireworks
It looks like a fountain
It lights up the sky
I like doing my name with sparklers
A firework goes up like a rocket
Fireworks are colourful
Fireworks make sparks
There's a Catherine wheel
I like pretty fireworks.

Katie Amos (6)
Olveston CE Primary School

THE OBDONGOODOO

The Obdongoodoo lives in a cave,
He keeps a person as a slave,
Long and worm-like is his tail,
His nose is like a slimy snail,
He has three needle straight strands of hair,
He has millions of teeth and some to spare,
He has lips like fire and two ice cold tongues,
He takes in twenty breaths of air straight to his lungs,
He has children for breakfast and adults for tea,
He keeps them in a cupboard locked up with a key,
He has a square shaped nose,
And long green toes,
His body's pink and fat,
He has ears like a cat,
He has short stumpy legs,
And lays orange eggs,
Now he's looking for his tea,
Ahh . . . He's going to eat me.

Jenni King (11)
Olveston CE Primary School

SHADOWS IN THE DARK

Shadows appear on the wall.
Shapes are changing as they pass.
The moonlight beaming through the blinds.
Now the shadows are getting smaller.
Then a small marching shadow creeping up to my bedroom.

But they will be all gone in the morning.

Joanna Sawyer (8)
Olveston CE Primary School

MY MONSTER

I have a monster
It's really gruesome,
It always follows me,
Now we're a twosome,
We went to see my auntie,
Who lives in Kent,
She won't let us back,
Because of the scent,
My monster's friend has slimy pink ears,
A gross sick-like scent,
It's big for its years,
Her big fat blue lips,
Her horrid green nails,
The eyes look like,
Two large brown snails.

And now I'm being followed by two,
'Oops sis', didn't know it was you!

Bethany Cottam (11)
Olveston CE Primary School

SPOOKY SHADOWS

Spooky shadows in the corner of my room.
Haunting shadows running around with a boom.
And in the shadows of the wall.
Don't look like shadows at all.
Other shadows I see too.
Without talking it makes them look like you.
Soon they will be gone, won't they?

Jenny Davis (8)
Olveston CE Primary School

THE THING

I saw it in the darkness, it gave me quite a fright.
It turned around quite quickly, but I was out of sight.
I ran into my room and hid under my bed.
I thought it was going to eat me but it turned around instead.
I popped my head around the door
I can't explain what I saw.
Gruesome eyes, gruesome nose,
Blood dripping down from head to toes.
I think it just ate my sister
It went to the bathroom and spat out her blister.
It jumped out the window and ran down the street.
Everyone heard its thundering feet.

Jack Houghton (10)
Olveston CE Primary School

NIGHT SHADOWS

S cary shadows in the night.
H aunting shadows in my room.
A ll the shadows in the gloom.
D aunting shadows playing tricks.
O utline or image on the wall.
W inding shapes in the moonlight.
S hadows from the night turn into day.

William Harper (8)
Olveston CE Primary School

PLANET EARTH

At the beginning and the birth.
God made the sun, the stars, the planets
and God made earth.
Now at first we appreciated it, loved it and cared for it.
From the water to the sand, in fact all over the land.
From the mountain to the range . . .
But then came the change!
At first we didn't harm it much.
Just a titchy bit, just a touch.
But then . . . we got *really* bad,
Were we crazy? Were we mad?
We filled the earth with horrible things
Who did we think we were, *kings?*
For years we crammed it with,
jobs, money, cars, shops, houses, gas, clothes,
pollution, paper, chalk, pencils, pens and ink.
I mean not once did we even *pause* to think,
that all these things weren't meant to be there.
The truth is we really didn't care.
But now our poor world is a disgrace
And we can't even look our *nice* God in the face!
And whose fault is it? Ours.
We're to blame, we're all horrible, we're all the same . . .
Well not all.
There are a group who want this treachery to cease.
If you want to know our name we're called
Greenpeace.

Alex Gardiner (10)
Olveston CE Primary School

PLANETS

Mercury and Mars
Are both quite red
Saturn and the sun
Are both a bright sight

Neptune is made of
Bubbling, bubbling water
But Uranus alone goes
Topsy turvy
And Earth is the only one with life

Earth goes round the sun
Moon goes round the earth
All the planets go round the sun
But Earth goes at a tilt.

Are there really aliens
In this galaxy?
Or are they in a different one
A different galaxy?

There are so many planets
In this universe
More than we can count
So let's stick to one
Stick to one
Stick to one galaxy.

David Thomas (7)
Parkwall Primary School

NIGHT OWL

Night owl, night owl
Owl in the night
Who had a flight
Oh night owl, oh night owl.

Night owl, night owl
Owl in the night
Who met a real knight
Oh night owl, oh night owl.

Night owl, night owl
Owl in the night
Who had a fight
Oh night owl, oh night owl

Night owl, night owl
Owl in the night
Who went to bed to get away
from the light
Oh night owl, oh night owl.

Justin Stabbins (8)
Parkwall Primary School

CORKY THE ORCA

Sharky, Stripe and Corky too
are all the same school of whales,
With their saddle patch behind their dorsal fin
but an orca called Keiko,
has an infection on his pectoral fins
All whales, dolphins and fish all live in water
They jump, they swim and they eat.

Paul Humphreys (8)
Parkwall Primary School

OUR SCHOOL

Our school,
It's 42 years old
Everybody works and plays
That's our school!

We have many visitors
That come to our school,
Bristol Rovers, musicians,
Animal carers too.
That's our school!

There are our teachers,
Ms Lyons, Mrs Pace
And many more as well
The teachers work and
Help us work too
That's our school!

We also raise money
For those in need of food
For animals that are endangered
Sales and competitions.
That's our school!

Thomas George (9)
Parkwall Primary School

WORLD POLITICS

Saddam Hussein is threatening
to blow up the world
with a bomb the size of a camper van
my, he must be in a whirl.

He is in Iraq
the English and Americans are joining forces
to have the battle
I can't wait till the war has ended.

It's so exciting
but sometimes it's frightening
they've got guns and bayonets
they've got everything galore
they're even in helicopters and planes.

Saddam Hussein has chemical weapons
so we threaten him
and get the SAS to blow up his weapons
and threaten the world.

John Goscombe
Parkwall Primary School

STREETS

Poor people on the street,
Nothing on your dirty feet,

Clothes in rags,

Home in bags,

Poor people on the street.

Benedict Ryland (10)
Pucklechurch CE Primary School

Pencil Case

Pencil case
Pencil case
Small one
Long one
Pencil and pen
Pencil case
Pencil case
Pencil case
Pencil case
Long rubber
Fat rubber
Ruler and
Sharpener
Pencil case
Pencil case
Pencil case
Pencil case
Long ruler
Short ruler
Cartridges and
Crayons
Pencil case
Pencil case
Pencil case
Pencil case
Pencil, crayons
Compasses and
Other shapes of
Rulers
Pencil case
Pencil case.

Michael Pike (10)
Pucklechurch CE Primary School

ROADSIDE TRAVELLERS

Far away from Bristol
In a lane not far from here
The air as clear as crystal
The hillside steep and sheer.

The verges are a vibrant green
The trees are full of nests
The birds that crouch and preen
The hedge is at its best.

The grazing sheep on the hills
The cows that are in the corner
Give the hills its added frills
As the days grow gradually warmer.

The evergreens and soft woods
The blossoms and the buds
Deciduous and redwoods
And a tiny pair of puds.

Trees, they are a life-giving plant
That helps you live and grow
Without them live we can't
Though they're growing rather slow.

So forget about wood panelling,
Decorations made from wood
Concentrate on recycling
That makes the country good.

Far away from Bristol
In a lane that's treasured dearly
The air is clear as crystal
And the memories remembered clearly.

Hannah Storey (10)
Pucklechurch CE Primary School

MONOPOLY

Mayfair is grand
Not as stylish as Strand
Park Lane draws the line,
Vine Street has the wine.
The car knows the rule
To the jail you fool
Land on a 'chance' it might be advance.
Old Kent needs your rent
You're an apple to buy Whitechapel.
The dice looks nice,
Euston Road has a pond with a big fat toad
Kings Cross is the boss
When it comes to Liverpool Station
But Piccadilly is a bit silly
Go past 'Go' and collect your salary
Trafalgar Square it needs a bit of care
Land on 'free parking' and the dog will bark.

Christopher Hounslow (11)
Pucklechurch CE Primary School

THE CAT

The cat stalked the night
Ready to pounce at a movement,
Moving swiftly across the shadows,
Noises are gone, the cat pads on.
There is peace.
The sun rises with an orange glow,
The cat's out of sight until nightfall.

Rosie Spencer (11)
Pucklechurch CE Primary School

ALL KINDS OF ANIMALS

In the countryside all kinds of animals rule the land.
The sky is clear and the forest is silent.
Then *bang!* Here comes a stampede running through the forest
damaging all of the beautiful wild flowers.
Suddenly squirrels start to appear,
they climb up trees and grab some acorns
and start to nibble away.
Then I can hear a noise, it's getting dark
and then some barn owls start to come
and they hide away in their holes in the trees.
With their eyes open they make a noise.
It's summer and all kinds of animals come to play,
even the skunks come to stay.
The antelope goes down to the lake
and fishes happily splash about.
So all kinds of animals are having an excellent time.
Especially all of the squirrels and the hedgehog.

Kelly Greening (10)
Pucklechurch CE Primary School

WEATHER

No matter whether the weather is bright or low,
Or whether the weather is happy or sad,
I know you'll always be the same.
No matter whether you'll rain or snow,
No matter whether the weather is strong or calm,
I will always like you no matter what weather you are.

Kirsty Siddons (11)
Pucklechurch CE Primary School

WAR

Boom! Bang! Bombs flying!
Machine guns firing!
Blood flying!
A festival of gore!
Aeroplanes dropping bombs!
Grenades being thrown!
Land mines exploding!
Soldiers flying through the air!
Dying, being shot!
Blood splatters everywhere!
One team has to win!
Tanks blowing up!
Missiles zooming through the air!
The city's all in wrecks!
Soldiers retreating!
Solders attacking!
Being shot!
Being blown up on land mines!
One team has to win the war!
Yes, one team has won!

Adam Evans (10)
Pucklechurch CE Primary School

THE BLUE SKY

I would like to have the sun rising in my bedroom
I would like to paint the sound from a bee.
I would like to put the moon in my pocket.
I would like to have clouds floating in my bedroom.
The sound of the waves swishing in the sky.
The white clouds carrying me into the sky.
I wish I could fly in the blue sky.

Mark Gapper (10)
Pucklechurch CE Primary School

MY LITTLE VILLAGE

In the park the swings are swinging,
And the roundabouts are spinning silently,
The birch trees rustle,
And the bushes hustle in the breeze.

The shops are shutting,
As the people finish work,
The pubs are opening,
And it's getting really noisy,
People are going home,
Sitting by the fire reading their homely magazine.

The little village church,
Rings its lovely bells,
As it strikes 8 o'clock,
People are all silent,
And are inside nice and warm.
I love my little village, it is my home.

Jilly Jones (10)
Pucklechurch CE Primary School

FRUIT

An orange is a fruit,
Like an early morning sun,
A grape is a fruit,
That has juice like a stream,
A banana is a fruit,
That sometimes is green like a tree top,
Or yellow like a mid-day sun,
A strawberry is a fruit,
Like a rose with stamen heads poking through.

Lee Blackwell (10)
Pucklechurch CE Primary School

I WOULD LIKE

I would like to put the Milky Way
in my pocket and touch the owl's song.

I wish I could see a star grow
in space and touch the rainbow
I wish the grass would dance for me,
if we could I would like it to touch my heart.

If we could, I would put the world
in a box and I would put the sun and the moon
in jar to keep in my cupboard.

Then I think I would get the stars and put
them in a box in my cupboard.

Thomas Adkins (10)
Pucklechurch CE Primary School

THE PANTOMIME

Learning my lines,
Learning my lines,
For the pantomime.
Learning my lines,
Learning my lines,
Learning them as best as I can.

Learning my dance,
Learning my dance,
Doing the movements wrong.
Learning my dance,
Learning my dance,
Nearly getting it right.

Alice Lewtas (9)
Pucklechurch CE Primary School

THE ROBIN

Robin, robin, bobbing along.
Sing your song, sing your song bobbing robin.
A sweet song he sang as he ran.

Robins, robins flying along
Sing your song, sing your song, flying, bobbing robins.
A sweet song they did sing they made my ears ring.

Robins, robins hopping along
Sing your song, sing your song, hopping, flying, bobbing robins.
A lovely choir they sung, the loveliest choir had just begun.

Dickon Wells (9)
Pucklechurch CE Primary School

KITTENS

The kitten is
rolling,
playing,
jumping.

In the garden
chasing his ball
climbing up trees.

Then in he comes
into his bed, sleeping
as the whole night goes past him.

Hayley Read (10)
Pucklechurch CE Primary School

WINTER DAY

Winter is that chilly time of year,
When Christmas is getting so near,
With ice-cold snow
and winds that blow.

It's a time to play in the snow
While fires give heat and glow
With snow crisp on the ground,
and people fooling around.
While ponds thaw,
people snore.
Next day the snow had melted,
Nothing left but a frozen puddle!

Stephen Gowing (11)
Pucklechurch CE Primary School

THE OCEAN

Dolphins dart left and right.
School of tuna get in a fight.
A shark comes, the fish will go, the shark goes
The fish will come back.
Whales jump up and down.
Stingray glide across the ocean floor.
Now the shark is back for its tea.
The ocean offers it a tuna but that is not enough.
It snatches a dolphin.
The fish will now come out.
A dark boat comes over,
The fishermen are here.

Amy Bush (10)
Pucklechurch CE Primary School

ANIMALS

Some animals are cute,
Some animals are scary,
When you go to touch them,
Some of them are hairy.

Some of them have stripes,
Fixed upon their fur,
When you go to touch them,
Beware for they might *grr!*

Don't be angry because they might bite,
Don't be angry because they might fight.

Some of them are short
Some of them are tall
Some of them are big
And some of them are small.

Jonathan Tucker (10)
Pucklechurch CE Primary School

KITTENS

A tabby kitten
playing,

Rolling,
chasing its tail around and around
jumping,
and darting up and down the room
running,
and biting laces off shoes in excitement.

Getting tired, lying down in a
curled up fluffy ball, softly purring.

Lauren Cockburn (9)
Pucklechurch CE Primary School

LAST NIGHT

Late last night,
When I went out,
I met the girl,
That this is all about.

Her eyes, they sparkled,
Like diamonds clear,
And a hoop, it was there,
Hanging from her ear.

Her ginger hair curled,
Like waves on the sea,
Late last night,
I was happy as can be.

She sat at a table,
Facing the bar,
As I walked up,
My thoughts were far.

Then she turned round,
And looked at me,
And when she stood up,
It was Terri Dee!

I had to say 'Hi!'
When she said 'Hello,
Aren't you that girl
From the radio show?'

Emily Graupner   (11)
Pucklechurch CE Primary School

ROCKS

Rocks, rocks,
Rocks everywhere,
Rocks on beaches,
Rocks in parks,
Rocks.

Rocks, rocks
Rocks, rocks,
Rocks *everywhere!*

Rocks on top,
All dirty and dusty,
Rocks on the bottom
All shiny and slippery.

Rocks on the side,
Shiny and bubbly,
Rocks on the other side,
Diamonds that shine.

Emma Newport (9)
Pucklechurch CE Primary School

THE UGLY ALIEN

There once was an ugly alien
who had a purple nose.
He walked down to the village
shop and tripped on his big long toes.
Birds went whizzing round his head
and pecked him on the cheek.
He went right home on his little
legs and went straight to his bed.

He woke up in the morning and brushed
his purple hair,
He walked down to the shop again
to buy a yellow pear!
But what he thought was some fruit
was really a little stone
And the little ugly alien went straight
to his planet, Tone!

Amy Tilley (10)
Pucklechurch CE Primary School

WIND, SUN, RAIN, SNOW

The golden sun sparkles and shimmers
upon the pond and seas.

Seasons come and seasons go
wind, rain, sun or snow.

The cruel rain comes down hard like nails
it wets the leaves.

Seasons come and seasons go, wind or snow.

The good wind has blown the rain away.
The wind is strong, it's blown the seed from their flower.

Seasons come and seasons go it's just snow.

The white snow upon the field has the power
to make plants and creatures sleep for hours.

Seasons come, and seasons come again.

Jerome Scholefield (11)
Pucklechurch CE Primary School

SEASIDE

The ocean roars,
The waves are cold,
Crabs hurry sideways and jellyfish sting.

The golden sand is turning brown,
The tide is coming in,
The people have fled and the beach is quiet.

Dawn is here,
The people return,
And the beach is full again.

Children playing,
Children paddling,
Everyone is having fun.

Zoe Davis (9)
Pucklechurch CE Primary School

THE BOY CALLED MIKE

There was a boy called Mike
who woke up on a load of lines.
When he woke up on that lovely fine day
he went out to play but he only had one friend
and he was a pen, he was called Fine Liner.
They were playing down the woods
but suddenly Mike sat on a pile of pine
and hit his spine.

Gareth Alvis (11)
Pucklechurch CE Primary School

THE CREEPY GRAVEYARD

As we are walking to the churchyard
Leaves are scattered on the floor
When we get to the churchyard
It makes me scared just looking at the door
We go through the gate
It's quiet and peaceful
Creepy leaves climbing up the wall
The bell is chiming
New gravestones shining
There's a creepy feeling in the air
As the wind lifts my hair.

Stacey Searle (10)
Pucklechurch CE Primary School

UNTITLED

Surprised at the news
Lots of packing to do.
Saying 'goodbye' to friends
And buying them sweets.
And giving them treats
Then there's the journey,
In the car for hours.
Moving van behind trying to keep up
Arriving, unpacking to do.

Ruth Evans (11)
Pucklechurch CE Primary School

WINTER GRAVEYARD

It was winter and the graveyard
Was as still as still can be,
I was walking there, when something big
Jumped out and frightened me.

Ten feet it was, but that's
Just height
It was sixteen feet wide
And when I saw it, my first impulse
Was to run away and hide.

I didn't though, I couldn't move
I was stuck in one place.
The monster seemed to recognise
The fear across my face.

'You're afraid' it said 'You mustn't be,
I'm not going to hurt you.
I need directions to the church
I was just about to ask you.'

'I'm sorry' I said, smiling at the beast
'It's just around the corner.'
And I ran back home before the beast
Had had the time to answer!

Jessica Wells (11)
Pucklechurch CE Primary School

MERRY BOXER

I am a merry boxer
I get into the ring
Wallop, wallop, thud! I go
Until the bell goes ding.

At first I lost the battle
Then I lost the belt,
I gained them all back again
And won a baby's rattle.

Tom Edwards (10)
Pucklechurch CE Primary School

KITTEN

I went downstairs,
She wasn't there,
I went outside,
I heard a faint miaow,
Then it was quiet.

I sat down, listen,
I heard it again,
I followed that miaow,
I heard something.
I didn't know what it was.

I pulled it out,
It was a kitten,
It looked ill and cold,
I took it indoors,
Out of the cold.

I gave it food and milk,
Then cuddled it close,
I heard someone calling,
The kitten went to that door
And miaowed,
I saw it with its owner,
And then I felt happy.

Gemma Louise Davenport (10)
Pucklechurch CE Primary School

COUNTRYSIDE

When I walk through the green fields,
I smell the country breeze,
I lie down and think,
Then see the cows and sheep.
The grass looks green,
The river looks blue,
I wish I could live in the countryside too.

The silence of the wind,
Is blowing really hard,
The river is silent,
It's getting really dark,
The wind has started roaring,
And the river has started crashing,
I wish I could live in the countryside too.

Amanda Dunleavy (9)
Pucklechurch CE Primary School

BEARS

Bears, bears, bears, everyone likes bears,
White bears, cuddly bears,
Fuzzy bears, furry bears, daddy bears,
Mummy bears, baby bears,
Big bears, small bears,
Funny bears, sad bears,
Grumpy bears, brown bears,
Cuddly bears, mummy bears
Big bears, funny bears.
Everyone likes bears.

Jodie Chilcott (9)
Pucklechurch CE Primary School

BITS AND BOBS OF THE BODY

B ones are odd and funny shapes.
I nside your body there is your heart.
T ummy rumbling makes me hungry,
S illy stomach is always rumbling.

A ll day your heart's pumping.
N oses help us smell.
D igestion is what happens to your food.

B lood runs through the body.
O xygen is good for us.
B ones we break are put in plaster.
S tomach rumbling when I'm hungry.

David Smith (11)
Rodford Junior School

BODY BITS

The heart pumps blood around the body,
The brain is the body's control centre,
The eyes make you see,
The liver sorts out the blood,
The kidneys filter the blood,
The hair grows on your arms,
The food in your mouth goes down the gullet,
The food goes to the digestive system,
The digestive system is all curly and whirly.

Tim Skuse (11)
Rodford Junior School

PIANO

I like playing the piano,
I've been playing for 2 years.
And in that time I've learnt few things
For it takes a lot of practice.

The notes I've learnt are A to G,
And I can play a lot of songs.

Jason Andrew Summers (10)
Rodford Junior School

HORSES

Horses, horses, horses are the best,
I could ride them north, south, east or west,
Horses, horses I love horses.
Brown bay reminds me of a sandy beach
With the crashing of the waves on the rocks.

Janie Porter (10)
Rodford Junior School

I LIKE ICE-CREAM

I like ice-cream
a whole lot
they taste good when days
are hot
in a cone or a dish
this will be my
only wish.

Scott Smith (10)
Rodford Junior School

WHEN I PLAY FOOTBALL

Every day when I play football
I give my friends a call
we all meet on the grass outside
and someone brings a ball.

I like to go in goal
to try to stop the ball
even though I'm that tall
I still can stop the ball
but that's not all the time.

I like being striker
because I like to score
and when the ball goes in the net
I like to score some more!

Scott Walker (11)
Rodford Junior School

FLOWERS

Pansy, daffodil, bluebell
All swinging in the sun
Like waving grass,
Swinging in the breeze
I like looking at flowers
I have them in my garden
Bright blue, sunny orange
Blooming purple.
My favourite colours.

Lydia Amesbury (10)
Rodford Junior School

THE NIGHT OF FRIGHT

The night is dark
it is a fright
there can be ghosts
and ghouls.
The full moon rises
and werewolves howl.

The night is full of fright,
it is scary in the night
it is full of scare and fright.

The wind is howling
the trees are blowing
The stars are a-twinkling
in the night of fright.

Jake Steeds (10)
Rodford Junior School

BEASTLY BUGS

Bees can be nasty, bees can be nice,
Bees can swarm so you'd better be nice.
Bees can help a lot so don't fiest.

Locusts are swarmers so they'll eat crops,
So don't come a cropper,
Locusts are robbers.

Bugs are real, bugs are cool and can be real carnivores!
Let some live, let some die,
Some can help you so don't fiest!

James Darren Templeton (10)
Rodford Junior School

BIRTHDAYS

Birthdays are full of fun
I love my birthday, it is always amusing
Are you looking forward to yours?
The presents that you will find
Hiding in a bag so you don't see
Do you love finding all of your things,
Are you always running and playing with your new toys?
I love my birthday so much I hope you do too.

Are you always wondering if it is jewellery
Rings or bracelets, earrings or bangles
Or if you're a boy, football things that you have asked for
Wait until the day has come.
You will have no idea what it is so have fun and wait.

So wait, wait, wait until the day has come
Then play, play, play with your toys so have fun on
Your birthday!

Clare Barnes (10)
Rodford Junior School

BE HAPPY

Be happy when you're sad
Be happy smelling flowers
Be happy when you're cross
Be happy when you scream
Be happy getting a present
Be happy having a friend
Be happy going on holiday
Be happy when you're in love.

Amy Messenger (9)
Rodford Junior School

SCHOOL POEM

I hate school
It's such a bore,
But,
I love school dinners,
They're a winner.

I hate school
It's such a bore,
But,
I love playtimes,
In the playground,
On the football pitch.

I hate school
It's such a bore,
But,
I like certain teachers
The teachers that are kind
And understanding.

I hate school
It's such a bore,
But,
I love it when I go homeward bound
To see my lovely hound.

Scott Perkins (10)
Rodford Junior School

ME AND MY MUM

M is for mum,
E is for excitable

A is for acrobat,
N is for natural,
D is for dinner.

M is for magic,
Y is for you,

M is for me,
U is for unusual,
M is for miracles.

Bethany Portingale (9)
Rodford Junior School

DISNEYLAND, PARIS

D isneyland is such fun,
I   t is for everyone.
S un, sun in its place,
N ice and hot for the race
E njoy yourself in the palace,
Y ou will be happy every day
L unch with your characters,
A little song from you to him.
N ice and soft as you cuddle,
D onald, Minnie and Mickey too.

Heidi Dracup (11)
Rodford Junior School

BEES

Yellow hive,
and sting spike,
must be a
bee.

Bumble bees,
die if
they sting
you.

Queen bees
are very bossy,
always
hungry too!

Russell Reynolds (10)
Rodford Junior School

FUNNY TIMES

Funny times are just fine,
We go around shops looking at
Clocks,
We go to zoos and what do we do,
We jump in ponds and sing songs,
We buy chips and turn them to
Slicks,
We lob stones at Mrs Jones,
We always miss but we don't care
But beware.

Ashley Matthews (10)
Rodford Junior School

THE HAUNTED GARDEN SHED

In the shed amongst the tools there's a ghost, a ghost, a ghost,
He's there all day and he's there all night that's the ghost,
the ghost, the ghost,
He's got a best friend whose name is Dracula, yes Dracula,
yes Dracula, yes Dracula,
They sleep all day and they work all night, yes they work all night,
Do you want to know where Dracula lives?
Well he doesn't live in a garden shed,
And he doesn't live in a swimming pool,
He lives under your bed, under your bed,
under your bed.

Beth Ainslie (10)
Rodford Junior School

YUMMY FOOD

I like curry it's very nice,
but sure enough it's better with rice.
I eat junk food every day,
but the trouble is I have to pay.

All I do is eat and eat,
I don't like popcorn because it's too sweet.
I like food no matter what,
if you gave me food, I would eat the lot.

I like food it fills my tum,
I like food it's yum, yum, yum.
I like chips yes I do,
they taste good all the way through.

Stephanie Biggin (11)
Rodford Junior School

RABBIT

Rabbits are small
Rabbits are big
Some can jump high
Some can jump low
Some have small eyes
Some have big.

And!

If you run they run
If you walk they hop
If you jump they jump
And if you are kind
They will let you stroke them.

They feel smooth
Some feel rough
They can jump fast
They can jump slow.

If you haven't seen one
Go and find one.

Jason Timbrell (10)
Rodford Junior School

WINTER POEM

W inter is here and the snow is here.
I cy cold in the snow.
N ow here comes white snowflakes
T rying to fall
E nergy is coming from the cold frost
R unning down, down, down and down.

Joanne Webb (12)
Rodford Junior School

THE DAZZLING SUN

The sun dazzling
on a merry morning,
animals are sleeping
there's not a sound,
not a tinkle you can hear.
The trees are swaying
to and fro.
All is tranquil,
all is hushed,
but then wait,
a buzzing sound,
a little cry for help you hear,
silence again.
Look around, you see a . . .
a fly caught in the spider's web! Struggling,
frantically pulling,
at last
it's free.

Daisy Townsend (10)
Rodford Junior School

WINTER

W   inter is here the snow is falling,
I   cy path the trees are bare,
N   ow comes snowflakes dropping down,
T   he cold has come, the sun has gone,
E   nergy is coming from the frost,
R   unning down to the ground.

Lorretta Smith (9)
Rodford Junior School

SHARK ATTACK

S lowly, silently, he swims through the water
H e eats big fish he eats dolphins, the crafty creature eats us.
A nd there are all kinds of these mysterious creatures.
R emember there is a mean one called the Great White
K illing a lot of fish all day.

A ttacks a boat and it sinks so he has people to eat
T hese creatures, beware,
T hey are out there.
A shark that bites lives in warm water like the Caribbean.
C areful when you go to hot places he likes tourists to eat.
K illing you with teeth so sharp.

Ross Aron Pollard (9)
Rodford Junior School

DISNEY POEM

D isneyland is such fun
I n and out the rides we go
S uch, such fun
N ice hotels all around
E veryone enjoys it
Y ou and me know it's great
L oud music every night
A nd we stayed in a nice hotel
N ow we are happy
D isney is exciting.

Michael Youdale (10)
Rodford Junior School

ALL OF THE ANIMALS IN THE WORLD

A is for ants that scuttle about.
L is for lion which is very proud.
L is for lamb it can be very loud.

O is for ostrich that runs a lot.
F is for fox that runs with a trot.

T is for tiger that goes 'growl!'
H is for horse that goes trot, trot.
E is for eagle which eggs it lays.

A is for autumn robin it goes 'tweet, tweet.'
N is for nest that an eagle can rest in.
I is for insects they scuttle about.
M is for mouse that lives in a house.
A is for April the time of year animals like.
L is for lazy that's the sloth.
S is for snake slippery, slimy.

I is for iguana that changes colour,
N is for new duckling a cute little fella.

T is for tail of a fox,
H is for hedgehog which is spiky a lot.
E is for elephant which goes bump.

W is for whale it goes splash.
O is for owl that goes 'tu-whit-tu-whoo'.
R is for rabbit when it goes hip, hop.
L is for leopard it has lovely fur.
D is for dog it goes 'woof, woof.'

Rosie Brind (9)
Rodford Junior School

SEASONS

Spring has just come now
Winter has suddenly gone away,
The sheep are having babies
The flowers are starting to grow,
The year is just beginning.

I love the summer it's the best
The grass is lovely and it's fresh,
The sun shines bright
Even in the night
So I can stay out late.

Autumn is such fun
You can play out in the sun and leaves
They crunch as you walk on them,
The air is fresh and there's lots of breeze
The leaves make me sneeze.

Winter is so cold and fun
Building snowmen all day long
When I go very cold
It looks so white and sparkly
The light makes it gleam.

Amy Louise Lewis (10)
Rodford Junior School

WINNIE THE POOH!

Winnie the Pooh and Tigger too,
Eeyore and Piglet
My floppy, cuddly friends,
Adventures in, out around
All across the countryside.

Christopher Robin
Looks after them dearly,
Even if they are only toys,
They're the best ones, I know.

Sarah Smith (11)
Rodford Junior School

ME AND MY BRAVE TEDDY BEAR

It was a dark night,
The moon shone bright,
But not for me,
I was filled with fright!
I longed for a drink,
Though it seemed miles to the sink,
I stepped out of bed,
And gave Teddy a wink!
I tip-toed across the landing,
Silent with heart pounding,
I crept down the stairs,
And into the kitchen,
The noisy old tap dripped,
Nervously looked, as I sipped
Then, cup in the sink, Teddy will do without drink,
I ran to the bottom of the stairs,
And nearly dropped my faithful bear
I looked up the stairs, and what should be there?
A big black figure, a human, or was it bigger?
Then something bright lit up her face and tum,
The bathroom light, revealed my mum!

Victoria Perks (10)
Rodford Junior School

WHAT IS THE SUN?

The sun is a big yellow fireball
It is an orange too nice to eat
The sun is a torch with a bright
Gold bulb inside.

Yellow, yellow nice and bright.

The sun is a pound of butter melting
In the sky.

Red, red, burning hot.

The sun is a Smartie shining in the sky
Yellow, yellow nice and bright.

Bright, bright colours shining yellow, red or
Orange.

Now the sky's lit up with bright sparkling
Colours.

Jade Sully (10)
Rodford Junior School

SUMMER

S   ummer is always scorching and blinding with sunshine.
U   nder the sun people sunbathe getting brown.
M   y friends are always outside playing with me.
M   e and my family go on holiday for a week,
                      my friends all miss us while we're away.
E   verything that is metal is boiling hot,
                      especially seat-belt clippers in cars,
R   ain hardly every falls until winter comes,
                      but that's a long way away.

Matthew Stokes (10)
Rodford Junior School

GHOST STORIES

G lee fills me,
H aunted house I see.
'O h let's wander in,'
S aid my friend Jim.
T o the door we went,

S uddenly we were in.
T errible ghost I see,
O nly *courageous* men dare to enter.
R un to the door it's so creepy in here,
I ran down the street me and Jim, our blood running cold.
E ager to get home
S ailing through the door, *a ghost I saw, a ghost I saw!*

Sam Milton (9)
Rodford Junior School

BONFIRE NIGHT

On bonfire night when fireworks glow
rocket and stars are something to show.
Catherine wheels and bangers go *whoosh!*
And something set fire to my mum's brush.
Don't put bangers in your pockets
or you will get a shock
bangers and bazookas
give animals a fright
better keep them out of sight
on bonfire night.

Nicole Cater (11)
Rodford Junior School

GRAVEYARD

Empty, spine-chilling, graveyard
Cold and misty, overgrown,
Too terrifying for words,
How I hate it there.

I stare out of my window
Ghouls flying, glad to be free,
People who have been murdered lie there.

Grey dirty gravestones
With moss creeping out of cracks.
Ivy creeping slowly and silently.

Leaves scattered on the floor
Blowing in the midnight moonlight.
I see the ghouls creeping,
Creeping, creeping back to their grave.

Jenny Roberts (10)
Rodford Junior School

THE ZOO

At the zoo there's all sorts of things,
There are tigers, lions and a bird that sings.
It's so much fun it's the truth, I'm sure,
You can stay there all day,
There's loads to explore.

You'll never get bored in the wildlife park,
But no need to worry they don't have a shark.
There is a really big pool of seals
Who have lots of fish for evening meals.

Charlotte Scaplehorn (9)
Rodford Junior School

SUMMER POEM

When the summer is out
People start to laugh and shout
Because it's summer.

Adults and children just want to run and play,
Because they just can't stand the pain because it's a lovely day.
The wind blows through your hair
Like a shimmer of hot fantastic flames.

Summer is also the time of love and friendship
Like adults having fun and children watching them run
As they lick an ice-cream.

Summer is the time of thinking of family and friends,
But most of all is that we have fun.

Summer!

Laura Parsons (11)
Rodford Junior School

MY MUM

My mum is short and thin with beautiful
Golden hair,
She has sea blue eyes and a beautiful
Clear skin.

Her dress code is all right but a little out
Of fashion.
Summer describes my mum the best of all
Like a rich golden apple.

That's my mum who loves and cares for
Me.

Sam Wiggan (10)
Rodford Junior School

A WINTER POEM

Winter is snowy, winter is cool
Winter is just like an ice-cream cone
Winter is fun children are playing in the snow
Wearing woolly hats and gloves.
Now it's time for me to go to play in the snow
Chucking snowballs at my friends
So it's goodbye from me,
I'll see you soon.

Lee Pullin (11)
Rodford Junior School

ANIMAL RHYMES

I'm a mole and I live in a hole,
I'm a bird and it's absurd,
I'm an otter and it's getting hotter,
I'm a bear and I've got a load of hair.

Aaron Buff (10)
Rodford Junior School

FLOWERS

Flowers can be purple, pink, yellow and blue too,
They make your house smell nice,
They bring out the spirit in you,
They make you buy twice.
In the summer they pop out in fields,
Flowers are always bright.
They always will hate shields,
Flowers are alright.
When the winter comes their petals fall gently on the snow.

Samantha Bulley (9)
Rodford Junior School

RABBITS

My rabbit hops around its pen
Twitching its nose
Wiggling its whiskers
Makes its little bobby tail go up and down
Its back legs make a thump as it hops around its pen.
It comes up to me and takes food and slowly
Hops back to its cage to eat it.
Then it comes up to me and nudges my leg
In his language he's saying 'Come and play.'

Catrina Seymour (9)
Rodford Junior School

UNLUCKY, WORLD WAR, NIGHTMARE!

I was in a war,
Not knowing which one.
Perhaps I was in World War I,
Or II and if I was lucky enough,
Might be World War III.
I pray it isn't number three.
I would surely be doomed,
Doomed or dead.
Out of far space I realised,
That it was a nightmare.
Definitely not a dream,
I think I prefer being punched,
Plus unlucky than to be in the dreaded
World War I, II or III.
By golly I like to be myself.

Richard Clark (10)
St Ursula's High School

SANTA

I can't get to sleep
I'm waiting patiently for him to arrive
Was that him?
No just my sister.
Where is he?
He should be here by now.

I heard a banging
Here he is.
The long red jacket, the black trousers . . .
It's Santa!

There were presents by the tree,
A thank you note for the mince pies.
He has arrived.
I can now rest easily.

Tom Parnell (10)
St Ursula's High School

THE DOG

The big brown shaggy dog runs along the beach.
As he swims in the sea,
His shaggy brown coat goes black.
The sea laps against his body
Then he swims back and shakes on the shore,
Showering the family with sand and salt water.
He then chases the seagulls until it is dusk.
He goes home at night and sleeps by the fire.

Samantha Hawkins (11)
St Ursula's High School

GIVING A MESSAGE TO A TEACHER IN A DIFFERENT CLASSROOM

In the noisy classroom
In school,
I can see pupils fidgeting
And others talking,
When the teacher says they're not
Supposed to.

'Have you come to give me a message?'
The teacher asked me with a stern voice.
I gave her a note that my teacher gave me,
And the teacher in the classroom read it.

The pupils in the classroom start chatting
And their teacher looked up and said to them,
'You know you are not supposed to talk.'
The noise died down and I went back to
My classroom.

Angela Wu (11)
St Ursula's High School

MY DAD

My dad's going to build a den
just for me,
Then he's going to build a new car
for Mum,
Then afterwards he's going to build
my sister a new rocking horse.

'Dad have you finished watching football yet?'

Maria Aviles (10)
St Ursula's High School

WHAT IS YELLOW?

Yellow is the sun that keeps me warm,
Corn is golden yellow,
I can see lots of this colour,
Autumn leaves.
Stripes on bees and wasps
Butter and margarine
Cowslips in the country
My English book
Sunflowers in my garden
Liverpool's away kit is yellow
And Brazil's
Roses are sometimes and sour lemons
A submarine
Half of my lunch box
Melons are greeny yellow
Chicks
The moon and stars in the sky are yellow.

Joseph Edwards (9)
St Ursula's High School

AT THE BUS STOP

At the bus stop waiting for the bus to come,
In the dreary winter, winter days.
Minutes seem like hours,
Five minutes have gone by, still it is not here,
Eventually it comes down the hill,
But no, it is the wrong bus,
Still waiting, ten minutes now,
Yes now it has come,
It has come, it has come.

Patrick Stirling (11)
St Ursula's High School

THE SUMMER SUN

The sun is like a golden lion,
Pouncing for its prey,
Playful, jolly and gay.

It's hot, burning, red today,
The lion's now looking for its prey
It bites the people
They scream with pain.

The sun's still happy
Floating in the sky, it's full now
Having eaten its prey,
All the people run away in pain
And anger for today.

Jennie Boorman (11)
St Ursula's High School

WHAT IS YELLOW?

Butter so sweet,
Buttercups looking like teacups,
The sun is shiny yellow,
Bananas curved,
Melons round like a ball.
Workbooks are yellow,
Submarines are long,
A baby chick making noises.
Daffodils look like trumpets,
Bees are striped
Round beads.
There are yellow kites,
Lemons tasting bitter.

Jonathan Wootten (9)
St Ursula's High School

SPRING

Spring is coming,
Hear bees humming,
See the flowers,
Nice and bright,
The sun is up,
High in the sky.

Spring is just around the corner,
Flowers are ready,
Start preparing,
The big celebration coming,
Baby lambs and baby chicks,
Are dancing around the fields.

Spring is here,
Everybody cheers,
Cards are sent,
Eggs are eaten,
We all love,
The big celebration.

Stephanie Pembury (11)
St Ursula's High School

PLAYTIME

I have to play alone at playtime,
No one asks me to play.
They say I'm weird because I like to work,
They say I can't play football.

I'm just a lonely boy,
Not even my brother's class let me play.
I just walk past the girls and they say
'Go away.'
Everyone makes fun of my freckles.

Adam Woodman (11)
St Ursula's High School

SPRING

The flowers grow smelling lovely,
The bees are buzzing everywhere,
Sun is shining,
Plants are growing,
Oh how lovely spring is here.

Eggs are hatching,
Chicks are coming,
Easter is on its way,
Now is the time for new beginnings,
And happy times in spring.

Cute Easter bunnies,
Bringing eggs in baskets,
Little children hoping,
They've got lots of eggs.

Trees, plants and flowers are growing,
Spring is coming to an end.

Everybody is cheering because,
It's summer!

Darius Zeinali (11)
St Ursula's High School

PETS

I once had a goldfish,
Its scales like a hoard of gold,
It swam in its bowl in a circle
A hundred times a day.
I once had a rabbit,
Its soft brown fur like a fleecy lamb's,
It nibbled the grass in our garden,
A hundred blades a day.
I once had a cat,
Its tabby coat like a tiger's skin,
It sat on the sofa and drank milk,
A hundred licks a day.
I once had a dog,
Its energy never-ending,
It ran around and played games,
A hundred times a day.
All my pets have died,
I suppose we all do someday,
We just go like 'that',
And join our King in the land of heaven.

Paul Clarke (10)
St Ursula's High School

SPRING

Spring, what a wonderful time it is,
Bees buzzing all around,
Pretty colourful flowers blooming,
Sun shining bright in the sky,

Fluffy baby rabbits hopping,
Squirrels collecting their acorns,
Butterflies flapping their big colourful wings,
Oh, what happiness it brings.

Sarah Chuk (11)
St Ursula's High School

IT'S RAINING

Plip plop plip plop,
the rain comes down,
it trickles down the pipe into the full
dark drain.

Children jumping up and down in
the puddles they get themselves
soaking wet,
mothers telling their children off
trying to get them dry.

Then the sun comes out again and
dries up all the rain,
children laughing and running around.
Suddenly a rainbow comes out
bright colours shining in the sky.
The sun goes down and children
get into their beds
it's been a long tiring day.

Rachel Williams (10)
St Ursula's High School

MY LITTLE COUSIN

I have a cousin,
His name is Tom,
He came today,
It's his half day,
I like Tom,
We all like him.

When he comes to play,
I play with him,
I love him and I hope you do too.

I wish he lived next door,
He wishes I lived next door,
Thank goodness he is moving house,
Because we might be together.

Marianne Mitchell (10)
St Ursula's High School

I MISS MY DAD AND HE MISSES ME TOO

I miss my dad,
He works away.
I miss him every single day
I see him at Easter time
Christmas and summer too.
He tells me 'I love you.'
If I could have a wish,
That one wish would be . . .
That my dad could work
In England as soon as can be.

Gabriella Rizzello (10)
St Ursula's High School

MY CAT JASPER

She's my cat Jasper,
The panther of the night.
She prowls about all day long,
Not stopping for anything
Except for a fight.

She's queen of the sofa,
There is no king.
The dogs hate her,
And Jasper hates them.

My life will not go on,
If she runs away.
She's the best cat in the world,
That's why she's my cat Jasper.

James Gibb (11)
St Ursula's High School

CATS

I really like cats,
Even though they fight with bats.
You never see them in tears,
And you never see them shake with fear.

They fight with dogs,
And also with logs,
They really hate bugs,
But they roll on rugs.

I really like cats,
I don't know why
It's probably because they're not in pies.

Anna Derrick (11)
St Ursula's High School

HAPPINESS

Happiness, the word says it all,
It can be a child playing with a ball.

Or it could be just the
Pleasure of seeing a toddler
Playing with his toys and
Making a laughing noise.

It could be the sun in the sky
Smiling down at you, starting a
Brand new day.

Or is happiness just, when you
Look forward to the future,
What will happen next?

Everyone has their own happiness
And that's for them to find out.

Justine Miles (11)
St Ursula's High School

SNOW

Snow is as white as the clouds,
Snow is as cold as ice,
On the trees, on the ground, snow looks
Just as nice.
With snow you can do all sorts of things,
Like building snowmen and having snow fights.
You can use it to build houses and all,
Snow is so nice.

Sam Guest (10)
St Ursula's High School

SPRING IS COMING

Spring is coming,
The bees are buzzing,
Look at the sun,
Its job is done!

The sun has risen,
The chicks have been born,
The lambs have awakened and are
Playing about in the fields,
The flowers, so beautiful and colourful.
Late at night
The stars are twinkling like little diamonds.

Everyone is happy.
Spring is around the corner!

Becky Richards (10)
St Ursula's High School

WHAT IS YELLOW?

The sun is yellow bright it keeps me warm a lot,
Buttercups swaying in the field,
The yellow yolk of an egg,
Sweetcorn is yellow too.
Pollen in the flowers,
A yellow apple crispy and juicy,
A banana curved.
A cute yellow chick,
A cake with custard on it,
Autumn leaves in the trees are yellow,
Sour lemons!

Rebecca Stallard (8)
St Ursula's High School

THE CAT

The cat tiptoes across the snow,
its eager eyes searching for prey,
jumping here, pouncing there,
doing everything quiet, so quiet.
Silently the cat moves round,
always looking for its prey.

It carefully tiptoes into the house,
the cat is there sitting on the chair,
as still as a statue,
never moving looking there,
waiting for his dinner,
it sits so peacefully,
looking around.

Now the cat is at his supper,
not moving, not looking around,
just concentrating on its food,
as if it had nothing else to do.

Asha Lane (10)
St Ursula's High School

MY SEASONS

I love it in the springtime
When the snow is off the ground
I walk around my garden
And flowers pop up from the ground.

In summertime the weather is hot
And the children play outside a lot.

I love it in the autumn
When the leaves fall off the trees
Red, orange and brown
Are the colours you will see.

Finally comes winter
It's a happy time for me
I wake up Christmas morning
And find presents under the tree.

Roisin Lewis (8)
St Ursula's High School

WAR

Bombing cities
Bombing places like England and France
You would not like to be there because
It really is not nice
I mean really not nice.
Trenches that are dirty
I mean really really dirty
You could catch a nasty
Disease in there.
I mean really really nasty
A big blackout.
I mean really really big
Soldiers getting shot
Blood going everywhere
All you can see is smoke.

Maxine Hobbs (9)
St Ursula's High School

WAR

As you run into the deadly war zone,
People die and cry for help.
You look at your army slowly dying,
And you want to help,
But the enemy is all around.
You're running so fast
The opposition's bullets are missing you
By the skin of your teeth.
Every night and day
The deafening sound
Of the bombs drop.
But when you have fought
For years and years guns get you in the end
And then you slowly drift away
And die just like the others.

Oliver Harding (9)
St Ursula's High School

SPRING

Spring means new life
Flowers come
Trees blossom
Babies born
Hopefully sunny
Hopefully not raining
But I don't mind what the weather's like
Because spring will come whatever the
Weather's like.

Tom Parsons (10)
St Ursula's High School

SPRING

The wind is here the wind has gone
And now it's time for a spring song.
The lambs will start to jump,
While the rabbits start to thump.

Now spring is here and new life grows
And it's time for small fluffy chicks to hatch,
The chicks, rabbits and lambs are here
The flowers they grow in the sun.

It's time for Easter, it's time for spring
And joy and happiness brings love.
The flowers grow while the birds sing
And the birds sing for spring.

Dino Marsigliese (11)
St Ursula's High School

WHAT IS YELLOW?

Bees and wasps buzzing all around me,
Banana yum! Lemon yuk!
Buttercups growing in the fields,
Sunflowers you get them big,
In farmers' fields you will see corn,
Yellow daffodils opening out,
Sunset shining down at me,
That keeps me warm and warm,
Chicks are ones that will be born,
With yellow fur all over them,
Children have yellow ribbons,
Yellow pineapples will be out to share.

Jessica Griffiths (9)
St Ursula's High School

WHAT IS YELLOW?

The sun is yellow and very hot,
The sand all soft,
There are sunflowers and roses,
Tulips and dandelions.
At school there's yellow pencils and folders,
Bees and wasps with yellow stripes,
They sting you sometimes!
The corn sways in the air,
Pollen in the flowers and melons to eat.
Ribbon and paper to decorate,
And yolk in eggs,
Bananas, lemons bitter, sweetcorn sweet and pears.
And the leaves off the trees are yellow too.
The honey is a golden yellow,
And yellow is a lovely colour to me.

Nikki Donovan (9)
St Ursula's High School

SPRINGTIME

S ummer is on its way,
P ansies and buttercups bloom,
R olling in the grass are the new lambs,
I   love spring when it begins,
N ever early never late I hear the cuckoo sing
G rains of pollen make you sneeze,
T ortoises wake up to the sun,
I   gloos melt in the sun,
M eadows flower with wild flowers,
E ver ending spring, summer is now coming.

Sophie Harris (11)
St Ursula's High School

WHAT IS YELLOW?

Yellow is a colour
Yellow is the sand
There's yellow chicks - I like them.
Bees and wasps have yellow stripes,
Bananas are yellow and curved.
English books are yellow as well
Melons and lemons all in a row
Ready to be sold.
Pears and pineapples are sweet and sour,
Flora is the colour of the sun.
Sweetcorn served on a plate
Fluffy chickens
And woolly jumpers
And buttercups swaying in the fields.

Kirsty Cropley (9)
St Ursula's High School

MOTHERS

Mothers are special,
they love you all the time,
and you should love them,
they always make your bed,
wash and cook for you.
Mother's day is coming up,
I don't know what I am going to do,
with her yet.
I will either take her out to the zoo
or to a restaurant.
Whatever it is I hope you like it Mum.

Rebecca Broughton (10)
St Ursula's High School

WAR

Gas flooding,
People dying,
Bunkers blowing,
People going sky high,
Shouting, screaming,
Everywhere,
Guns going bang! Bang!
Soldiers marching,
Tank attacking,
Aeroplanes flying,
With big tears dropping,
Land-mines blowing.
Bushes burning
People tripping over barbed wire,
Blood squirting everywhere,
I hate war.

Tanzil Ahmed (9)
St Ursula's High School

RABBITS

Rabbits go around all day,
Doing nothing much at all.
Their little noses go up and down,
Gobbling up lots of grass.
Rabbits hop, up and down
Going in their holes,
I wonder if they enjoy their life,
Because they don't do much at all.
At the end of their day
The sun goes down, for another day.

Daniel Gough (10)
St Ursula's High School

WHAT IS YELLOW?

Yellow is the colour of the sun that keeps me warm,
Infants singing Yellow Submarine.
I like yellow paper but not bananas,
Corn growing in the fields,
I'm writing in a yellow English book.
Yummy custard and lemon sorbet,
Presents tied with a yellow ribbon.
Melons, pears and lemons are yellow fruits,
I have blonde hair,
Autumn leaves as well.
Daffodils, sunflowers and cowslips.
The stripes on wasps and bees,
The Brazilian football team shirt.
Yellow is a primary colour as well.

Chris Ashcroft (9)
St Ursula's High School

SPRING

Spring has just begun,
New life, new things, new everything,
Bobtails bobbing through the air,
Bunny rabbits everywhere.
Flowers everywhere you walk,
Baby chicks about to talk,
Little lambs being born,
Then fields are full of golden corn.
The frost has gone, now it's thawing
And morn has come, the day is dawning.

Kylie Gallagher (10)
St Ursula's High School

WHAT IS YELLOW?

What do you see in a field that is yellow?
Flowers,
Daffodils like drums,
Girls wear yellow ribbons,
Peppers, lemons and pears to eat.
The sun is hot and yellow,
Egg yolk,
Our English books.
Corn to eat,
Some sweets,
Even roses,
Also chicks, they are cute,
Dandelions are yellow and give a white sap.
There are so many yellow things.

Jason Battles (9)
St Ursula's High School

SPRING

Spring has sprung,
And the grass has risen,
Lambs are born in fields of flowers,
Flowers are flowering on the ground,
Tadpoles are born and
The sun comes up
And the hibernating creatures are
Walking around again.

Alex Rosengren (9)
St Ursula's High School

THE YEAR TEN THOUSAND

What will it be like in the year ten thousand?
Hover-cars flying. Perhaps the earth has been
destroyed or life has been destroyed or life has
been extinct for two thousand years.
No one knows.

I wonder if flying restaurants will serve you at
your home. Perhaps there's a swimming pool
in every home. Perhaps the buildings tilt from
side to side. No one really knows.

Will the earth be polluted by cars and smokers
or rubbish on the street and muddy newspapers
lying on the floor?
Probably they don't have streets.
No one knows.

Tom C Wardle (11)
St Ursula's High School

WAR

War is bad! Very bad!
People are flying, people are dying.
Guns loaded, peopled *exploded!*
One nation is dying, one is winning.
It's sad to think that they risk their
Lives just for land.
Soldiers were slaughtered,
People were tortured,
War is bad! Very bad!

Thomas Montgomery (10)
St Ursula's High School

SPRING

Spring is nice
Spring is sunny
Spring makes me feel all funny
I like to see lambs leaping
And I like to see butterflies flying
And birds singing
Their special sound.

Luke Hobbs (7)
St Ursula's High School

SPRING IS HERE

Spring is quiet
Spring makes me sunny
And the trees are often as peas.
Spring is like a dove
I like butterflies sleeping
And lambs leaping
Spring is everything above.

Jordan Woodman (7)
St Ursula's High School

A BOAT AT THE SEA

A boat was at the seaside
And the sea-water was fast.
The water went over the sand.
The sand was completely gone
Only the crabs were left.

Francesca Marland (7)
St Ursula's High School

WHAT IS YELLOW?

The sun is yellow and keeps me warm
Butter on my toast
Daffodils looking like little trumpets
Baby chicks at Easter
Custard on my cake
Mustard is yellow and I don't like it
Bees are yellow, striped like a zebra
English books are yellow too!
The blackboard ruler long and straight
Sand all over the beach
My woolly jumper that's on me now.

That's yellow!

Alex Falconer (9)
St Ursula's High School

WHAT IS YELLOW?

Yellow is the colour
Of the morning sun,
Fruit is yellow too.
Yellow is the colour in-between the
Black stripes on a bee
Flowers have yellow pollen
You can get yellow wool.
Our English books are yellow,
Melons are yellow,
Yellow is the colour of a submarine.

Lauren Fensome (8)
St Ursula's High School

ICE-CREAM

I like ice-cream it's cool to eat
I like ice-cream it's nice to eat
It's best to eat it in the spring,
When everything's at its ping.

Everyone is singing
Everyone is dinging and flinging.
Spring makes you spring
And jump and hump
It's lovely spring is.

James Hemmati (8)
St Ursula's High School

WHAT IS YELLOW?

Bananas are yellow and submarines,
Ribbons and English books.
Yellow chicks playing in the yard,
Yellow melons and pepper to eat.
Yellow sand and blonde hair,
Margarine is yellow and butter and lemons.
Sweetcorn shiny and hard,
Paper is yellow.

Ben Bracey (9)
St Ursula's High School

AT NIGHT

When I get home from school it begins to get dark.
I know it is night. I hear birds 'Good night good night'
I hear my rabbits scuttle into their hutch.
Owls scare them 'Twitter twoo twitter twoo.'

Mice scuttle along the gravel path 'Eek eek.'
And the horrible rat who lives in my garden comes
Out and steals food.
I get into my bed all cosy and snug,
And watch all the lights in the city go out.

Good night!

Millie Colwey (8)
Sefton Park Junior School

SNOW

The snow falls to the ground
Giving a soft wintry sound,
The ground is like a carpet of snow,
Sometimes the snow is dark and rough
And sometimes the snow is thick and tough.
Snow can be dangerous, snow can be bad.
Snow can be happy and snow can be sad.
It hardly ever snows, but then again who knows?
It could snow this year or the next,
Or the next,
Or the next,
Or the next . . .

Loren Lewis Cole (9)
Sefton Park Junior School

ANIMALS

An awful lot of animals live in different places
None of them have the same faces,
If they did it would get in a muddle,
Mostly in a very big huddle!
An awful lot of animals live in different places,
Luckily none of them have the same faces!

Cecily Evans-Blondel (8)
Sefton Park Junior School

THE SUN

The sun is bright
The sun is pretty
I like the sun, the sun is witty
The sun comes out when it is light
The sun goes to sleep when it is night.

Jade Templer (8)
Sefton Park Junior School

SCARED

I'm scared of monsters creeping around,
Slithering slimily on the ground.
I'm scared of spiders day and night,
Walking around they give me a fright.
I'm scared of snakes the ones with stripes,
They give me nightmares and they give me frights.

Daryl Allen (9)
Sefton Park Junior School

A POEM ABOUT MY BEST FRIEND

My best friend is Franklin Groege
his house is nice and warm.
He's got a great big garden,
he's helpful and kind.
I wish he could live next door
he's the best friend in the world.
His best sport is football,
he doesn't like athletics as
much as football.
On January 28th most people
were accusing him of doing something
he didn't do.

Marlon Lorenzo Gayle (8)
Sefton Park Junior School

MY RABBIT COTTONTAIL

My rabbit Cottontail is only five months old.
She hops around all day,
And when I go and get her
From outside she kicks me.
Sometimes she bites me,
But I know she loves me
And I love her too.

Annabel Wilson (8)
Sefton Park Junior School

SCARED

Scared of the dark, scared of spiders,
Scared of . . .
What's that? My heart is thumping up and down
I'm hearing whining, screeching noises
It sounds like, like a creaky floorboard or
A scraping door
I wonder what it could be.
I wonder
It's getting closer and closer
It's coming in
Ahhh
Oh, it's only my mum.

Mercedes Villalba (8)
Sefton Park Junior School

FLOWERS

I like flowers, I like flowers,
My favourite one is poppy.
I like flowers, I like to pick them,
I like flowers, I like all sorts of flowers.
I like flowers, I like flowers,
I like garden flowers, I like wild flowers.
I like flowers,
And then there's the powerful red rose flower!
I like flowers from different countries.
I like flowers, I like flowers.

Alice Eddie (8)
Sefton Park Junior School

POP BOTTLES

Pop bottles,
Pop bottles,
In a pop shop,
When pop bottles pop,
Pop bottles pop.

Fizz in your face,
Is a disgrace,
When pop bottles pop.

Pop bottles,
Pop bottles,
In a pop shop
When pop bottles pop,
Pop bottles pop!

Gemma Gray (11)
Summerhill Junior School

PUPPY LOVE

I had a dog which was my friend,
Now the hurting will never end,
For now you lay still under the willow tree,
Where we used to play just you and me
Where there the good times we remember
Also the sad time of November
That was the month when you died
That was the month when I cried,
I cried and cried till my heart was bare
But I love you so and you'll always be
        There!

Laura Summerhayes (10)
Summerhill Junior School

IN SUMMERHILL SCHOOL

In Summerhill school,
There are lots of bad boys
And lots of good girls.
The teachers shout,
And the children scream
And Mr Galliott keeps them in.
Then we do some spellings and handwriting,
Then Miss Ridsdale reads us the BFG.
Oh no! The bell has gone for home
And then I tell my mum what we have done.
I say we've done some spellings and handwriting,
And then Miss Ridsdale reads us the BFG
And then the bell went for us to go home,
And that is all that we have done.

Ayisha Grant (8)
Summerhill Junior School

THE DRAGON

My dragon's back is like a green village
Because of its hills of grass
And its eyes are like sapphires burning.
His wings are like giant leaves.
His roar is like thunder
And his feet like cathedrals.
His nails are like shining swords.

Ashley Porter (8)
Summerhill Junior School

PORTRAIT OF A MONSTER

For his back I'd need a green town,
For spikes I'd use rhinoceros horns,
His tail would be a brick wall,
For his eyes emeralds burning,
And his head would be the front of a car.

Alec Cridland (8)
Summerhill Junior School

PORTRAIT OF A MONSTER

For his back I would need to go to Egypt to see a pyramid,
For spikes I'd use lots of sharks' fins.
His tail would be gold with bright shining crystals on it,
As for his eyes - they would be stones and rocks.
His head would be a gigantic red light,
His legs would be skyscrapers and his arms would be trees,
His body would be a big circular clock.

Carl Winstanley (9)
Summerhill Junior School

MY MONSTER

My monster has wings like fluffy clouds,
        teeth like spikes in the sun.
My monster has a tail like a river,
        claws as sharp as jaws,
        eyes like dangling flowers,
And for his head a waste-bin.

Charlotte Evans (9)
Summerhill Junior School

HORSY DEVOTION

I'm going to miss you,
I'm always going to.
My friend, my dear,
Losing you was my greatest fear,
You're going to a different place,
An owner with a different face.
Will you forget me?
You're the key to my heart,
They can't split us apart.
But now you're gone,
I'll miss you,
So long!

Kyli Morgan (10)
Summerhill Junior School

A PORTRAIT OF A MONSTER

For his back I'd need green grass,
For spikes I'd use giant pyramids,
His tail would be a rope,
For his eyes I'd use two apples,
His head would be made of a big egg,
For his ears I'd use two clocks,
His teeth would be lots of swords,
For his earrings I would use lots of round hair bands.

Anna Francis (8)
Summerhill Junior School

MY MONSTER

My monster has eyes like *emeralds*
that sparkle in the dark.
My monster has wings, like when dolphins splash.
My monster has teeth like spikes in the sun.
My monster has skin as soft as fluffy clouds.
My monster has claws as sharp as jaws.

Jenna Webley (9)
Summerhill Junior School

A PORTRAIT OF A MONSTER

For his back I'd need a green hill.
For his spikes I'd use golden jewels.
His tail would be a rope.
For his eyes clock eyes.
For his nails shining swords.
And his head would be a lady's hat.

Tina Coombes (9)
Summerhill Junior School

A PORTRAIT OF A MONSTER

For his back I'd need a giant brick.
For spikes I'd need pyramids.
For his tail I'd use a long piece of string.
For his eyes emeralds.
And his head would be a box.

James Harty (8)
Summerhill Junior School

PORTRAIT OF A MONSTER

For his back I'd need a lumpy hill,
For his spikes I'd use shark fins,
His tail would be hundreds of people all playing tug-o-war,
For his eyes I'd use pools of sparkling water,
And as for his head - well I don't know -
Maybe a great big school.

Anna Phillips (9)
Summerhill Junior School

A PORTRAIT OF A MONSTER

For his back I'd need a giant pyramid.
For his spikes I'd use stingers.
His tail would be a cat's tail.
For his eyes I'd have red eyes.
And his head would be a giant head.
His tongue would be a red tongue.

Richard Bower (8)
Summerhill Junior School

MY MONSTER

My monster's eyes would be sparkling gems,
My monster's head would be a box,
And it would be green like the body.
His tongue would be a dead snake, again green.

Kirsty Inker (8)
Summerhill Junior School

A PORTRAIT OF A MONSTER

For his back I'd use
a house painted green.

For his spikes I'd use
sharp diamonds that twinkle in the sun.

His tail would be a rope that
slithers in the dark.

For his eyes shining gold that
sparkles in the night.

And his head would be the front of
a dolphin.

Georgina Cox (8)
Summerhill Junior School

PORTRAIT OF A MONSTER

For his body I'd need a big green hill,
For spikes I'd use lots of fir trees,
His tail would be a lake in the sunshine,
For his eyes I would need two glittery sparkling diamonds,
And his head would be the front of a car.
For his tongue I would use a dead red snake,
For his legs I would use four tall buildings,
His teeth would be rhinoceros' horns,
For his claws I would use eight little pyramids sparkling gold.

Rocky Hopkins (8)
Summerhill Junior School

THERE'S A DRAGON UNDER THE SEA

Right down at the bottom of the sea there is a dragon
looking at me.
He's *big*
He's *green*
He's *nasty*
A dragon!
He's come to land, whatever shall I do I've only got two hands.
He's *stinky*
He's *fat*
He's *big*
He *just needs a smack!*
So look our right down at the bottom of the sea,
there is a dragon looking for a girl just like *me.*

Rebecca Knight (8)
Summerhill Junior School

HALF PAST THREE

At half past three,
you go home for tea,
and the teachers say they plan for tomorrow.

I don't really think,
when you go home for a drink,
the teachers talk for an hour.

They must talk to friends in space,
and take their mask off their face,
and then turn into the *ugliest* person
you've ever seen!

Eugenie Brain (9)
Summerhill Junior School

WHEN I WAS IN THE PARK

As you walk past the river
and you're looking around
and something starts to bubble
from deep within ground
and you want to scream
when nothing comes out
and you run out
when you shout
then this time something comes
out and the ground cracks
faster than you so you put
yourself on full speed
and you zoom past
everything starts to blur.
When you are at home
you see your mum and dad
come down as skeletons
and you scream.
You wake up and you say
'Phew glad that was a dream'
then it all starts over again
you run out of your bedroom screaming
out from the front door
when your mum and dad are
laughing.
So when you go in the park
be careful or you will get a
          fright!

Matthew Owen (7)
Summerhill Junior School

IT WILL HAPPEN

As I walked softly across the dry ground,
My mind fluttered into the sorrow sound.

He lay as silent as can be,
I thought as he lay, what it would feel like to me?

He lay there looking calm and peaceful,
His flame extinguished, his body dull.

He was not at the dark end of his life,
He has a child, and a lovely wife.

I think as I pass, how will I die
And I think, why?

How do people live when they know of death?
I hope I never die.

Teri Gauge (8)
Summerhill Junior School

I HATE . . .

I hate Hallowe'en
Because I have to dress up.

I hate Noddy
Because he is for one year olds.

I hate Summerhill
Because I have to walk to school.

I hate being naughty
Because I get steps.

David Lock (8)
Summerhill Junior School

SCHOOL FRIENDS I'VE LEFT BEHIND

I had some very best friends in the infants
But now I've left them behind,
Because they've gone to another school
And I can't help but cry.

Their names were Ayisha, Kari and Adam
And they never never told a lie,
I really really wanted to see them again
But now I don't mind.

I keep on thinking about them
And I cannot sleep at night
But if I could only meet them
I'm sure I'd be alright.

Natalie Hart (8)
Summerhill Junior School

A SIMILE POEM

As wet as water
As woollen as cloth
As good as gold
As sharp as a knife
As green as a garden
As slow as a snail
As dry as a plum
As nice as a cat
As cold as a fridge
As hot as the sun
As fat as a van
As high as a flower
As big as a monster.

Rebecca Flanagan (8)
Summerhill Junior School

I HATE . . .

I hate sharks,
Because they're slimy.

I hate Miss,
Because she's a maniac.

I hate my brother,
Because he beats me up.

I hate football,
Because it's boring.

I hate spiders,
Because they're creepy.

Sam Bracey (8)
Summerhill Junior School

THE EMERALD GREEN SHARK

The emerald green shark is long and thin,
It slips round rocks,
And lives in a decorated cave,
He shimmers in the water.
He likes eating coral,
The emerald green shark is playful,
He's never greedy or horrible to others.
He sleeps in a blanket of crystal and gold,
In fact, he's the king of the sea.

Jake Edwards (8)
Summerhill Junior School

AS FAST AS A TRAIN

The boy was as good as gold
As blue as the sky
As cold as ice
As sharp as a pin
As light as a feather
As smooth as silk
As green as grass.

Kurtis Pinkett (7)
Summerhill Junior School

MY FAMILY

My family are sweet
they give me things to eat.
My brother and mother
are just like each other.
Me and my dad always
play football.

Christopher Takle (8)
Summerhill Junior School

THE FACE OF A PRINCESS

Her lips are like a red red rose,
Her cheeks are touched with pink,
She has the most prettiest hair of all,
And her skin as white as snow.

Laura Sanders (11)
The Park Primary School

WITCHES

W itches gliding
I   n mid air,
T   errible smells,
C   heeky cats,
H   orrible hags,
E   vil witches,
S   limy spells.

Hannah Palmer (10)
The Park Primary School

ABC

Annoying Anita always arguing,
Bob Bogus blaming Bossy Beatrice,
Chatterbox Charlotte chatting again,
Deane the Dob dobbing again,
Extraordinary Edward passing exams,
Funny Fred fooling around,
Gutted Gus gave gasping Georgia a gift.

Jordan Cara Mitchell (10)
The Park Primary School

SIDNEY THE SNAKE

Sidney the snake,
Is intelligent,
Drowsy all day
Tucked up nicely
In a warm bed of luxury,
Eddie his friend
Bounces up and down like a yo-yo.

Georgie Collier (11)
The Park Primary School

COSMIC SPACE MONKEYS

Shattering shuttles
plough powerfully past poor pale planets
aiming at astronauts.
Catching comets and colds
eating elephants while excited explorers explore.
Manky mad monkeys
observing orange planets madly
no more monkeys left.
Killing cods, they deserve what they get
eating apes is sick and rude.
Yet I miss those manky mad monkeys
and I don't have anything left to do.

Luke Loveridge (11)
The Park Primary School

ANIMAL MADNESS

Amazing leaping laughing leopard,
Hanging hairy monkeys,
Roaring biting lions,
Hissing like mad cobras,
Slow sloppy sloths,
Big grey water squirting elephants,
Colourful peeking parrots,
Hairy horrible tarantulas,
Stripy mad tigers,
Furry skinny ostriches,
Cute fluffy barking dogs,
Big mouthed smooth hippos,
Naughty small koala bears.

Simone Biggs (11)
The Park Primary School

IF I WERE!

If I were a butterfly I would fly very high.
If you were a bird in a tree would you sing
a tune to me?
If I were a great big bear, would you run away
or would you not care?
If I were a fox, hunting in the rain,
would you run away again?
If I were a human dancing in the street,
would you pay me a visit if we ever meet?

Elizabeth Feltham (10)
The Park Primary School

SOUNDS

Shh! I can hear a noise what is it?
It sounds scary. It sounds like a ghost!
Oh no what are we going to do?
Come on let's run.
But we heard it again
But it was different
It sounded like this 'Oooooooooooo'
And Tonia was whispering to me
And it got even louder.
Then we ran as fast as we could
And it was still following us.
Then we ran home
But then we found out
It was a real ghost.

Jahra Haque (8)
Twerton CE Junior School

COLD ICE-CREAM

Ice-cream is cold it melts in the sun
I like it because it tastes delicious and
Is very sticky
You can get it in a cone
You can lick it for ages
You can eat it at a table
You can eat it anywhere.

Jenna Williams (9)
Twerton CE Junior School

A FLAME A FLAME

A flame a flame jumping about
Up and down left and right
Round and round
They are yellow red and orange
They twist and twirl round and round.

Mathew Bayliss (9)
Twerton CE Junior School

I'VE GOT A FRIEND

I've got a friend called Jim
When I want to talk to him
I say 'Hey Jim'
That's how I know I am talking to him.

Jason Norris (8)
Twerton CE Junior School

FIREWORKS

Fireworks, fireworks, bang bang bang!
Sparkle crackle bang bang bang!
Beautiful colours twirly whirly twisty twirly
Whistle screech they reach the sky
As fireworks fly.
Fountains, fountains, beautiful fountains
Go up and go bang bang bang!
Beautiful colours, red, gold, silver, purple,
Glittery blue, screamers, Catherine wheels,
Rockets Bang!
Balls of fire explode
Dangerous dangerous fireworks are dangerous
Whoosh up go the fireworks, bang!

Lisa Tugwell (8)
Twerton CE Junior School

FIREWORKS, FIREWORKS

Fireworks, fireworks
They go bang and they explode
Fireworks, fireworks
They spin around
And they blow up everything.
Fireworks, fireworks
They burn your fingers
And they sparkle.
Fireworks fireworks
Go up in the air
And they are beautiful
Colours.

Daniel Skipp (9)
Twerton CE Junior School

FIREWORKS

Fireworks they go crackle zoom crisp and twist,
They scream and make loud noises.
Children scream and jump up and down.
Their mum and dad go up like a rocket,
And when the fireworks go - 'Wo!'
Children go 'Whee wow cool!'
Everyone says that was
        Amazing!

Emily Tanner (8)
Twerton CE Junior School

DOGS AND CATS

Dogs and cats love to play
Someone comes and takes them away.
The coppers come and rescue them
And take them to the RSPCA.
But some animals aren't as lucky as that
And they don't treat the cats and dogs properly.

Kirsty Lewis (9)
Twerton CE Junior School

SUNNY DAYS

Sun sun
Sunny day
I like sunny days
Sunny days make the
Daffodils shine very colourfully.

Christopher Townsend (9)
Twerton CE Junior School

SOUNDS

I can hear cars going past
Brum brum brum
I can hear ghosts shouting
Woo woo woo
I can hear Chris chatting away to Daniel
Chat chat chat
I can hear a police car
Nee naw nee naw
I can her a train
Choo choo
I can hear a dog barking
Woof woof woof
I can hear a baby crying
Wa wa wa
I can hear a cat miaowing
Miaow miaow miaow
I can hear the wind blowing
Woo woo woo
I can hear the clock ticking
Tick tock tick tock
The clock struck 6 o'clock
And I went to the chip shop,
Yum! Yum!

Tyson Lane (8)
Twerton CE Junior School

CRUNCH! CRUNCH! CRUNCH!

When I woke up this morning
I looked outside
When I had got dressed
I went out.
There was snow on the ground.
When I walked round I heard
Crunch! Crunch! Crunch!
The wind was blowing through the trees
So I went in where it was warm.

Hayley Piper (9)
Twerton CE Junior School

SOUNDS

I hear footsteps when kids walk and run
I hear cars when they're going fast
I hear people talking and tapping on the table
I hear the trees blowing
I hear the sea moving
I hear the animals barking and howling
I hear Miss Watts writing with her pen
I hear Jason's watch beeping.

Danny Hulbert (9)
Twerton CE Junior School

SOUNDS

Quiet! Quiet! I can hear drip sounds
                Drip! Drip!
Quiet! Quiet! I can hear a scary sound
                Oooooo!
Quiet! Quiet! I can hear a sound
It sounds like a mouse - tweet!
Quiet! Quiet! Tweet!
You can hear 6S scribbling,
And some horses clip clopping,
And Jahra And Tonia, chatting,
And the bell ringing for lunch.

Camille Brown (9)
Twerton CE Junior School

FIREWORKS

Fireworks twirl and twist at the end or the start
They all go *bang! Pop!* Crispy crackle in the sky
You'd better mind they don't go in your eye.
The people go 'Ooo! Look at that! Isn't it pretty?'
They spread out in the sky and they leave a trail of smoke
Balls of fire go up really sharp and then at the end
They spread out into sparks.

Emma Harding (9)
Twerton CE Junior School

SOUNDS

Tuesday, music teacher says if we are quiet
We can hear
Birds chirp! Chirp! Chirp!
Horses clip! Clop! Clip! Clop!
Mice squeak! Squeak! Squeak!
6S working scribble! Scribble! Scribble!
Me breathing
Jahra and Sarah whispering whisper! Whisper!
Then we all hear ooooooooh
We all stare at the door!
But it is 6G swimming in the pool.

Tonia Kays (9)
Twerton CE Junior School

I KNOW A MONSTER

I know a monster very mean
I know a monster red and green
I know a monster who's very tall
I know a monster who's very small
I know a monster who's called Sampson
I know a monster who's very handsome
I know a monster who likes honey
I know a monster who's very funny.

Lewis Fishlock (8)
Victoria Park Junior School